THE CHALLENGE OF
CHANGE

LIVING LIFE AS BEST YOU CAN

GAIN STRENGTH IN FAITH
EDWARD CONINE

Copyright © 2022 by Edward Conine

All rights reserved. No part of this book may be produced, scanned, or distributed in any printed form or electronic form without permission. Although every precaution has been taken to verify the accuracy of the information contained herein, the author and publisher assume no responsibility for any errors or omissions. Some names and Identifying details may have been changed to protect the privacy of individuals.

Printed in the United States of America

Book layout: BookBaby.com

Cover design: 99 designs

The Challenge of Change / Edward W. Conine
1st addition

ISBN (Print Edition): 978-1-66786-876-9
ISBN (eBook Edition): 978-1-66786-877-6

TABLE OF CONTENTS

INTRODUCTION 1

HOW TO CONSIDER CHANGE: CHAPTER ONE 5

TOPICS AND STORIES: CHAPTER TWO 15

THE GRAPE FROM GOD: CHAPTER THREE 57

UNDERSTANDING WISDOM: CHAPTER FOUR 119

CHANGING TIMES: CHAPTER FIVE 127

SOCIAL HISTORY / SHARING ALONE TIME: CHAPTER SIX 159

GOD'S LOVE IS DIVINELY PASSIONATE: CHAPTER SEVEN 189

INTRODUCTION

Change is personal, often diverting our status quo. Some changes are routine and decisions are easily resolved. Others are more difficult because they demand a new direction in change of a more challenging situation. World change is more of an abstract consideration for us; as we adjust to our own environmental daily routines; hoping to have comfort in our personal progress. None of us can predict all changes, which occur in every day life; meaning, there are ones that surprise us with an unresolved problem, effecting our demeanor, sometimes shifting us into a frightful circumstance. These tragic events can be brutal and long lasting, often leaving us with a shattered spirit, sometimes with no return. Having faith, that is agreeable to us, is important. Where faith comes from; is sometimes confusing to us, trying to find where to put our faith. There are numerous religions listed in this presentation, along with historical empires, human development, interesting scientific observations, and the historical progress in our existence. My intent is to expose my version of Christianity, as a powerful source to live by. The Bible is proven by its truth, because of prophesy; predicting events long before they actually happen, as the power of its truth is revealed at a later time. Mankind has the gift of intelligence to rule over everything this planet provides. Many theories have attempted to explain why we are here? From Creation to the space age; there has always been a God. He calls Himself the Alpha and Omega… the beginning and the end.

THE CHALLENGES OF CHANGE

HOW TO CONSIDER CHANGE:

CHAPTER ONE

There is always something in the presence of life, distracting us from our comfort zone. The action we take, will settle our soul, or turn us away from reality or peace. Considering suffering and pain, individual choice is the key to success or failure. Change can include others in similar situations, but the single recipient, adapting to change, is the final judge, leading to resolution or not. Pain and suffering, without a cure, is the lowest level of life humans can endure. This event unfolds without previous planning or direction. The individual participants find themselves in a surprised dilemma of how to find stability and comfort. Feeling trapped, with no way out, is a common first reaction to unwanted changes. Medical intervention is the first goal in stabilizing the body. Over time, the physical aspect of change will stabilize; but then what are we left to cope with? Adapting to compromised independence, we learn there is no going back. Most of us are willing to use resources, as best we can, seeking stability in their new condition. Reaching satisfaction will come when you modify and acknowledge the results of change, then battle for a satisfactory outcome. There is a need to identify changing demands; beginning with adjusting to things you can do, rather than dwell on the things you cannot do. Considering pain and suffering, or actually living under its burden, each one of us will experience the hopelessness and sorrow in this frightful situation. Our ability to find resolution, compromised strength and endurance, is to focus on adapting and adjusting to these altering events. My personal history adjusting to pain and suffering, is to focus on the event; the time it will take to recover or not; and how the change will effect my lifestyle, Then using motivation toward recovery, 'I accept the final results.' At the age of seventy-nine keeping up with physical events that were normal in the past, now threaten my lifestyle, altering my activity. At this age, there is no going back. The question is what happens next? Newly diagnosed, with complications from back surgery six years ago, eventually leading to a continual, mild to moderate pain, I have tolerated the discomfort during those years. However having notable change in discomfort, I contacted our family Doctor who recommended getting updated X-rays. The result noted; a fracture and some change in a stabilized a slipped disk, that shows two broken titanium screws resting in my spine. I remain active, doing as much as I can, including lifting objects I should avoid. But now I am waiting to visit my surgeon to reveal what can be done without surgery. Hoping to avoid more discomfort. This has taken several weeks to evaluate and receive the surgeon's recommendations, pending on results of tests. Thinking the pain is not severe enough to have surgery, I am beginning to think of the immediate future and how it will effect the remainder of my life on this planet. Truly believing in God's promises, and willingness to love me, I stay close to Him in prayer and supplication, knowing there is a better life ahead of me. Unresolved pain effects my independence. Caring for my property, fixing things that are broken, and the simplicity of grooming our lawn and garden, are past routines of ease, now leading to a burden of failing physical abilities. Trying to meet my goals, in active toleration is short lived, as

I require additional physical effort. in completing tasks. Discomfort effects, shortening the task at hand; then working in short bursts of time, avoiding heavy objects, seems to be the best I can do. In my younger days doing projects, was to press on until fatigue, then stop.

Today, it hurts before I even start! . Toleration is minutes, rather than hours. Pain relief is accomplished by rest, and the use of appropriate medication, along with the good sense to avoid over taxing physical abilities.

Pain reduces quality of life: Pain can bring a remarkable change to our demeanor and thought process. Attempting to do small projects while in pain, effects my focus, often causing additional disturbance in coordination. If I don't monitor the situation, it can lead to discouragement, producing anxiety or anger. Being uncomfortable, makes it difficult to concentrate on what you are doing. Extending time to complete the job, or give up altogether; is always an option to consider.

Control in Suffering: Our ability to concentrate on the positive things under our control, helps our suffering become tolerable. Accepting medical relief through surgeries, physical therapy, and controlled medications, may help ease physical pain; but our emotional wellbeing, depends on our willingness to compromise for stability. As we contribute as best we can, the negative part of our personality may not be encouraging to others, and should be subdued. Remaining calm, is a comfort to those who are committed to helping with your ailments, as best they can. Nothing is profitable, when we snap at our caretakers, and family Your comfort depends on their care, so be grateful for their interaction and extend your thankfulness for their efforts. As a believer in the Bible; I think of this…Jesus Himself overcame brutal physical pain, verbal degradation, and torment to set us free from the sinful environment we live in. His sacrifice on the cross, and His reaction to it, is enough for me to know… God understands pain and suffering. It is up to us to accept our future, no matter what happens next. Compromising situations are common in everyday life. Most are easily resolved choosing between several options. However, with abrupt physical change, options are limited producing a prolonged period of anxiety, until motivation and acceptance are confirmed.

Encouragement from Jesus: 2 Corinthians 1:3-5 NKJ " "Blessed be the God and Father of our Lord Jesus Christ, the Father of mercies and God of all comfort, who comforts us in all our tribulations, that we may be able to comfort those who are in any trouble, with the same comfort which we ourselves are comforted by God. For as the sufferings of Christ abound in us, so our consolation also abounds, through Christ". **Matthew 6:34 NKJ** "Therefore do not worry about tomorrow, for tomorrow will worry about its own things. Sufficient for the day is its own trouble".

Tolerance: There are many who live with the burden of pain, which cannot be cured by a single event of surgery or medications. Therapy, and short lived pain interventions, gives relief for a short time, but need to be repeated frequently. Most of those experiencing these conditions, find some additional relief through diversion. Distracting ourselves using tactics away from concentrating on pain, is one way in finding short relief. Using humor as a good diversion in difficult situations; by looking at the bright side of life, away from my discomfort… is welcomed. There is always something in the presence of life, distracting us from our comfort zone. The action we take, will settle our soul, or turn us away from reality or peace. Considering suffering and pain, individual choice, is the key to success or failure, can include others in similar situations, but the single recipient, adapting to change, is the final judge, leading to resolution, or not.

Medications: Pain pills should not be used as a supplement to increase activity, but remain in there are designated requirements for comfort. After a physical event, prescribed pain may not be enough to overcome the time period, when unrelieved there may be a tendency to use more. Controlling pain relief with mediations is normal, but we should also avoid dependence, beyond the required recommendations. Finding something to use for safe relief of discomfort, pharmaceutical considerations may be the first choice, but they are limited to a designated period of time. There are many other available possibilities in pain control, without being addicted to drugs. The disabled and the elderly, are very aware of comforting techniques. This is when we learn to adjust to what we can do, and avoid what we cannot do, to remain stable. There are many who live with the burden of pain, that cannot be cured by a single event of surgery or medications. Therapy, and short lived pain interventions, only give relief for a short time, but the need to be repeated frequently, is evident. Some of those experiencing these conditions, find some additional relief through diversion, using tactics shifting away from pain gives relief in demeanor Although, they experience unresolved pain, in their attempt to find a diversion to overpower their discomfort, focusing on valuable gifts in life, that led to pleasant comfort in the past.

While working with patients in the hospital setting, having family or friends at the bedside for longer period of time; is a gift that enlightens all involved. Working in intensive care is very busy and limited in short visiting periods. Some of my peers criticized my techniques, having visitors stay longer than the visiting rules. However, when experiencing situations in suffering, the need for comfort is a positive force toward reality and peace, and family and friends are welcome to provide positive interaction toward recovery and peace. Considering suffering and pain, individual choice is the key to success or failure. Change can include, others in similar situations, but the single recipient, adapting to change, is the final judge, leading to resolution, or not. Challenges in life, will bring focus toward your determination, endurance and motivation. Adjusting to abrupt mental or physical conditions are the most devastating of all. The elements of individual choice is paramount in taking action, adjusting to the change; accepting a new direction, is not easy. Two things come to my mind when change occurs… Truth and Proof.

Truth: as a noun: "That which is true or in accordance with fact or reality, or a fact or belief that is accepted as true". **Proof** as a noun: "'The action or process of establishing the truth of a statement, or A series of stages in the resolution of a mathematical or philosophical problem.

Adjustments: In this world of kaos, it is not easy to find the best resolution for your comfort. How to find the best response in a time of change, burdens the recipient with emotional threats that may need to be resolved, before receiving stability. . Relying on others, using available resources toward resolution, the question is; can we be satisfied with group decisions, or disregard those who sincerely want to help? Without help from others, how would this process of life look like?

Change is like using stepping stones, that lead to the Kingdom of God in Heaven. Some stones provide a solid foundation, while other stones are unstable… allowing an occasional slip or fall. When falling, we make the decision to pick ourselves up, or remain where we are. When unable to rise, we welcome others to help us reestablish our balance. My hypothesis is to remind us, the world is complex, divided between good and evil. Personally I spent the first three decades of my life in trying to gain success by the powers according to this world, unfortunately my mission lacked the need for God's help. To my surprise thirty years of knowing God exists, but not communing with Him, my daily life, by world standards…suddenly shattered. My goals toward success, failed miserably, sending me to the darkest point of my life; devastating my pride to the point of no return. Without hope, my life, fell into darkness. Troubled with extraordinary circumstances, it seemed I had no where to go? When reaching out to God, during my lowest point, my faith needed correction, in understanding the presence of God's Holy Spirit'. Pondering what the Holy Spirit meant surprised me because of being baptized in the name of Jesus Honors His life, death, and resurrection; but the saving grace from sin, is found by understanding His blood sacrifice on the cross, too believe and follow His sacrifice for our redemption .At the age of ten, believing, without maturity, I did not know His salvation comes from our Heart, not from water baptism. Believing in Jesus from our heart, His Holy Spirit is given to us as a counselor aspart of our triune God. Leading us in the right direction that produces the promised everlasting life in Heaven. The Holy Bible is the only source, explaining the good in life as we know it". We are here, temporary, in the form of the flesh, which is housing our true self as spirit. The Bible leads us to the promise of everlasting life, beyond our physical death, as we believe God is real, understanding from our heart, His love, showers us as an eternal being. The Spirit He gives us.; guides our path leading to His Kingdom, as we simply believe in Jesus. His book has much to say about a Creator who made this world and everything in it. Life as humans, are lost if we do not recognize the power of God, and except His Son Jesus as our savior. Now guided by the Holy Spirit, my faith is in Jesus alone. Through the simplicity of His calling, we confess our belief in Him in truth, connecting to God, through the Holy Spirit; regardless of being baptized, or not. Jesus is the answer to life beyond this world. Known as the Surpreme Being, God offers the gift of ever lasting life, as we believe in Him. God allowed the life, death and resurrection of Jesus Christ, to demonstrate the process of life after death.

History of the world linked to the Bible: The history of the world, is connected to the historical truth found in the Bible. As we challenge the direction of love, over evil, I'm so grateful God overlooked my stupidity. By acknowledging His love, to those who love Him back, is our free choice to claim; Jesus as our Savior! Then follow His lead, in 'Truth and Proof: Also, the emotional state of the unknown, is combined with the question of 'what to do next?' Anxiety plays a big part as we pursue choices toward believing God or not. **2Corinthians 4:17-18 NKJ:** "For our light affliction, which is but for a moment, is working for us a far more exceeding and eternal weight in glory, while we do not look at the things which are seen, but at the things which are not seen. For the things which are seen are temporary, but the things which are not seen, are eternal." Why is it, we focus on things we see, and ignore what we cannot see? The future is not known until we have lived it. Change effects our lives, and our ability to adjust or not, hoping for a comfortable existence. The most important part reducing my anxiety, is consumed by my faith. God is far beyond our comprehension, but has written a book… The Bible. Using forty authors, in three continents, with profound truth, the validity; this book is the answer to the gift of life. Given from God., who expresses the true meaning of love, to identify the mystery of our existence; using His underlying premise… too 'Love First', above all other things. After reviewing many religions, I find the God of the Bible, wants us to love 'Him'. Why? Because He loves us, just as He loves others. Our goal is to be at peace, then bond together in consolation, like a 'Family'. However… there is a spiritual battle effecting us all… the choice between good and evil.

Health and Wellness: As a retired nurses, my wife and I combine over eight decades of nursing care in a hospital setting. The value in our background gives us the opportunity to be directly involved with patients experiencing difficult times…some with dismal outcomes.

Adjusting to change: is a combination of the multiple choices we make each day.. Our choice will effect our future. Most variations of change can be resolved with little effort. However, some changes, need careful consideration to be resolved, while others are left without resolution. Health issues, accidents, world wide disasters, crimes, war, and unusual events, are in the news every day. Most of us ignore anything that does not apply to us, attempting to maintain our status quo. The ability to survive in unresolved situations, is critical. Finding stability and acceptance in difficult times, is paramount in our ability to thrive. Rejecting help from others or avoiding your individual responsibilities, will lead to failure and dismay. The key to success, is to overcome change you cannot resolve, by adjusting to the results that remain. We are all created equal, but many of us miss the opportunity to thrive, without understanding the will of God. No matter what your environment provides, the promise to live in paradise forever comes with the single choice to believe in Jesus Christ and be saved… or deny Him and be lost!

Know this: Nature, history, personal challenges, and believing in the God of the Bible, are led by examples of hope. Hope is to improve self-realization as you work through changing events, using every resource available to find resolution. The best approach toward stability and truth, is to establish confidence. Those of us, who have the means to adjust, need to be aware that compromise is a necessary component toward stability. Accepting loss, in exchange for stability, is of greatest importance, to satisfy all who are involved.

Life Changing Events: During our career as nurses, my wife and I have been honored by the opportunity to see hero's in action…"patients and family enduring hardships and sorrow". The ability to endure times in strenuous situations, is a difficult task for all of us. Success or failure is always present in the attempt to find stability. Each event of change, challenges us to focus on a solution. There are some situations when guidelines are helpful, but not fitting to the need at hand. The outcome of any event will rest on individual responsibilities and choice, seeking to find the best results.

TOPICS AND STORIES:

CHAPTER TWO

Presented as remarkable circumstances, designed to share success or failure in change; Disabilities and Old age; Physical and Medical Dilemma; Chronic Health Issues; Terminal illness; Trauma; Substance Abuse; and Impending Death; are a few examples of change to consider. Many challenging situations, out of our control, may change our thinking to a different way of perspective of living. Emotional, physical, and mental capabilities, are key to finding stability, during altering events. With most serious situations, there is no going back to normal. The goal of overcoming inevitable change, is to use compromise and acceptance, when approaching a different direction to life. The following examples of Traumatic Events and Stories of battling change, are shared to give a glimpse of struggles in real life situations. Being in the center of attention, does not always imply to a single individual, but includes adjustments of change, to all who are involved.

Conception to Birth: As a nurse, spending six years in the field obstetrics, I enjoyed the process of birthing. The sound of a new life, crying to fill their lungs, often gave me chills and occasional watery eyes. However, one day I was having a conversation with an Obstetrician about our growing children. Unfortunately, I was not guided by faith; leaving God on a shelf, when the words from my mouth reflected…

if my daughter ever got pregnant, she would have an abortion!" The Doctor's response was... you do not have that choice, it is hers alone! Not too long after that conversation, a pregnant teenager came to be examined, accompanied by her mother. During our conversation she quoted she was going to keep her baby and was excited to be a Mom. Preparing for the baby to be at home, was almost accomplished, and both her and her mom, were happy with the circumstances. During the pre-exam, I discovered the absence fetal heartbeats. The doctor was notified and came quickly to the exam room. Unfortunately, the baby had died in the womb. Explaining the process of inducing labor, to birth her lifeless child, the mother asked if she could hold her baby afterwords? Proceeding with the delivery process, preparation for viewing was completed. As I held this tiny human, walking toward his mother, I was unable to hold back my tears and sorrow, as the three of us grieved together in the loss of this precious life. This event changed my stupidity, in agreeing with abortion to remove a mistake, in favor of strongly believing 'it is a murder of convenance', rather than a life giving responsibility!

Birthing: The life of a child starts at conception, progressing as a fetus, until birthing is accomplished. Neonate is a term for infants living their first year of life. Not all survive after conception and there are some who are challenged physically, after birth. These two categories provide research and the advancement of medical intervention to assure growth and wellness during the birthing process. After birth, adjustments may be needed to stabilize a disability. If an abnormal change happens, all involved, (parents and professionals) are challenged to adjust to the need of this new life. Depending on the circumstances, some are more complicated than others. The goal is to provide direction for everyone. For some parents having a compromised child, there is need to support them, with confidence. A special child can be a burden, or a reward toward the receiving parents. In retrospect, observing many situations, almost all involved, are willing to commit to the challenges ahead.

Having Faith: Believing we are accountable to God in life or death, it is difficult to understand why we must go through trials and tribulations. It is notable we can fail on our own, not realizing we need help. Seeking a suitable resource is an important compromise or resolution, leading to stability. In times of struggle, it is like a person trapped in an Airplane falling to its demise; it is a wonder what each person is thinking, in their last moments of life. Let Your Will be done on earth as it is in heaven"; is part of the Lords prayer, giving us comfort trusting God for all things; especially in short lived moments and critical events. There is nothing we can do, without trusting God's loving will, guiding us through all kinds of difficult circumstances. The reward of living with God in paradise, is our ultimate goal. As a believer, it is paramount that I commune with God on a personal level throughout the day, as often as I can, no matter what occurs. Even sometimes using 'inappropriate language', as my emotions get the better of me. God is ever present, no matter what! As He examines your heart to see if you truly believe in Him, and accept His presence. If so, He offers everlasting life in His kingdom for those who commit to His loving presence. Believing in Him; we are able to live our life with the hope and promises, waiting for the new life to come, through Jesus. However those who refuse God, will be lost because they do not know him. The question is do you know Him?

Critical Changes: The following topics and stories, are a few memorable circumstances designed to share success or failure, to control dramatic changing events, effecting the direction of our lives. Unusual events require faith, hope, endurance and trust. These examples are presented by real life situations, sometimes beyond our control, struggling to find stability, satisfaction, and acceptance.

Decision In Child Bearing: Steve and Angie: Met each other at Calvary Chapel Church, in Boise, Idaho 2001. Their common attraction to their friendship was to follow a healthy life style. Angie stated she first accompanied Steve in exercise, because he had all the gadgets to keep track of their data. Pairing as a couple in exercise, they eventually they fell in love, grew deeper in their relationship, then married in 2003. During the first two years of marriage they had not conceived. Seeking medical advice, it was discovered that Angie needed to stimulate her ovaries, using follicle stimulating hormones. For some women, pregnancy is far from the biggest issue in their lives, but for others, it is getting the egg fertilized that is the hard part. There are oodles of reasons why it might be difficult for women to become pregnant. Women who wait, it is often age, that hinders them. Female fertility starts to decline by age 25, by the time a woman is 31, her fertility drops by 3 percent annually. There's a group of women who might have a depleted egg reserve, also other times it's a thin uterine lining. Sometimes, it might even be the male factor in infertility — which accounts for 30 percent of all infertility cases. Fortunately, many causes of infertility can be diagnosed. Technology has become advanced enough that we can actually fertilize embryos outside of the human body and place them into the womb hoping for a positive outcome. Parents who have struggled with infertility or keeping their pregnancy, are grateful for these interventions. Still, there are challenges to infertility and the treatments that come with it. Adding synthetic chemicals to the body does pose some risks, and there are risks to the pregnancy, to the baby, to the mother, and to the father. The likelihood of a miscarriage is higher with fertility treatments, as well. Other outcomes may not happen suddenly. Instead, the treatments used for couples facing infertility, may predispose them to a greater likelihood of trouble down the road, such as birth defects or chronic conditions which may develop in the mother and impact her for the rest of her life.

As important as it is for many couples to have a baby, these factors should be considered at the same time, especially if fertility measures don't prove to be effective in the first few rounds. Adoption is a way of compensating the desire to have a Family. Love has no bounds in rearing children from another mother. Many scenarios have led to happy lives from this process.

Trying to find the best way to conceive, Steve and Angie contacted a fertility expert to guid them through this process, (we will call: "Dr S") Questions? What happens if I have to little of follicle stimulating hormone? In women, a lack of follicle stimulating hormone leads to incomplete development at puberty and poor ovarian function (ovarian failure). In this situation ovarian follicles do not grow properly and do not release an egg, thus leading to infertility. Experience suggests that there are main risks associated or potentially associated with the hormone treatment used in ovarian stimulation; ovarian hyper stimulation syndrome, questionable cancer, and effects on future fertility. In the ovaries of the female reproductive system, an ovarian follicle is a fluid-filled sac that contains an immature egg, or oocyte. During ovulation, a mature egg is released from a follicle. While several follicles begin to develop each cycle, normally only one will ovulate an egg. How many follicles should each ovary have? On average ten to twelve follicles are produced per cycle, but this can vary from person to person and is affected by multiple factors such as age, medical history and your individual response to ovarian stimulation. Do multiple follicles increase the chance of pregnancy? The risk of multiple pregnancies after two follicles increased multiple deaths or disabilities. Therefore more than two follicles, are considered High Risk for birthing After much discussion in reviewing this process, Steve and Angie were willing to move forward using the two follicle approach.

Unfortunately, the identification of being pregnant with five embryos were noted, instead of just two. In this situation there is a much higher risk of complications and death to the fetus or the mother. The safe approach in this situation is to abort the pregnancy, to save the possible death of the mother, then start all over. After being notified, 'Dr S' recommended termination using a D&C (dilation and curetting) to remove the contents of Angie's uterus, and start over, due to hyper stimulation with complicated threats of defects or death, because of multiple embryos.

Broken in spirit, what to do? Believing life begins at conception, all follicles were now imbedded as embryo's, being stimulated to grow until birth. To abort the life within her, was out of the question for Angie; even if her own life was threatened. This single commitment speaks volumes in the fact that life begins at conception. Steve and Angie selected the sovereignty of God to speak for themselves, as they put their trust in His will, praying for an answer. This information came on a Friday and they were left to decide what to do, over the next week. They prayed for guidance and noted their church was finishing up the "Sanctity of Life Week" on Saturday evening. They attended and prayed for all unborn babies, along with their congregation, and pondered the dilemma they were experiencing. After this service, in the comfort of their home, they decided against the D&C; in favor of continuing with the pregnancy. Trusting in God's will for their lives. Leaving the five embryos to the outcome of this event; trusting God's power and strength; they found peace in their decision to carry on.

The following week, they turned away from their present 'Dr S' in favor of an Internal Fetal SpecialIst in multiple births; "Dr K."

Who was selected for his expertise as leader in multiple birthing. Dr K. re-emphasized the probable high risk results, then gave them some time, to be sure of the possible consequences, before they committed to this unpredictable outcome. He assured them, no matter what their decision, he was all in, to accomplish their needs. Finding peace to bring life into this world, even under the most difficult circumstances, echoes our national motto "In God We Trust." What a great witness to those of us on the outside looking in, knowing some of us might remove this problem before it begins. Steve and Angie are true believers in the God who made them. It is by His power they rest…even with the possibility of death, or disability.

John 16:21 NKJ "A woman, when she is in labor, has sorrow because her hour has come; but as soon as she has given birth to the child, she no longer remembers the anguish, for the joy that a human being has been born into the world".

Having no regret, they found peace in their decision. Steve and Angie, prepared for the event, praying for the best possible results. They found value and comfort in the following verses: -**1 Corinthians 3:6-7 NKJ;** " I planted, Apollos watered, but God gave the increase. So then neither he who plants is anything, nor he who waters, but God who gives the increase" . Adding the scripture from the book of Proverbs, gives another example of their faith.-**Proverbs 3:5-6 NKJ** "Trust in the Lord with all your heart, and lean not on your own understanding; In all your ways acknowledge Him, and He shall direct your path."

Hard Road Ahead: Can a baby survive at 21 weeks? Babies born under 21 weeks did not survive, even in cases where medical treatment was provided. The typical survival rate for premature babies born at 22 weeks ranges from 2 percent to 15 percent and is "an uncommon event," according the National Institutes of Health (NIH). Can a baby survive at 22 weeks if born? The study, involving nearly 5,000 babies born between 22 and 27 weeks gestation, found that 22-week-old babies did not survive without medical intervention. ... But for 22-week-olds, he said; we don't have enough to offer the babies, a reasonable chance of survival.

Medical Viability: According to studies between 2003 and 2005, 20 to 35 percent of babies born at 24 weeks of gestation survive. While 50 to 70 percent of babies born at 25 weeks survive. Then more than 90 percent born at 26 to 27 weeks, survive. Also, it is rare for a baby weighing less than 500 g (17.6 ounces) to survive.

Preparing for the birthing process: Beginning with five embryos, the first consideration is to maintain is appropriate nutrition until labor begins. For most Mom's, producing enough nutrition for one child or even twins, it is natural to consume more nourishment through the process of being hungry. However, with multiple embryo's, additional nutrition above natural consumption is needed. The requirement for Angie was to consume 5,000 calories per day, which led to a weight gain of 100 pounds, when delivering at 24 weeks. In comparison; The Air Force Academy requires 6,000 calories per day for the cadets, because of the intense challenge of physical training.

Preventing early contractions: The most critical part of this pregnancy is preventing early contractions. The minimal goal is to reach at least 24 weeks in gestation, as the time to deliver, for the survival of the fetus and the safety of the mothers life. However, knowing the possibility of this happening without complications is evident. Bedrest was ordered to prevent early contractions, but at 15 weeks having early contractions, a cerclage (purse string suture) was placed to help prevent cervical dilation. A contraction monitor was also ordered, and medications given to prevent labor. Noting: all of the above, information given from the doctors, in the beginning; is now becoming a true in reality.

Hospitalized / Time to birth: At 21 weeks, the contractions got worse and hospitalization was required. Angie was admitted to the hospital for closer observation and care. On May 26,2006, with thirty eight people present in the delivery room, (doctors and attendants prepared to accept each new born) and the challenge began! Having five separate stations with equipment and supplies... the process began with a caesarean section, then moving each neonate to its prepared station for immediate medical treatment. Each fetus, now being recognized as neonates, we're quickly assessed and treated, then taken to the Neonatal Intensive Care for further advanced medical treatment. As mentioned in the beginning, survival would be costly. Of the five, two will survive, and three will perish.

Babies: Luke, weighed 1 pound 13 ounces and passed 8 hours after delivery; Kate weighing 12 ounces followed Luke within that time period; One month later; Ashley weighing 1 pound 3 ounces at birth; passed with inadequate survival complications; Mary, weighing 1 pound 5 ounces, thrived and was discharged home; at 36 weeks after conception (3 months after birth). Lyndsey weighed 1 pounds 6 ounces, needed more time than Mary, to pass breathing requirements. She was discharged a month later; (4 months after birth). Not forgotten: Each child was named, and the ones who passed are not forgotten. Cremated, and housed at home, in their urns, is a reminder they are with God, expecting to be reunited as a complete family in Heaven. In the beginning of this venture, Steve and Angie, accepted the two follicle approach to birthing. However, with the revelation of five embryo's, learning the extreme complications of survival, even death, they refused to terminate fertilized eggs, which are the beginning of life. They were convinced God's power and grace, would accomplish His will through their faith, and He did!

Now, fifteen years later Mary and Lyndsey are thriving teenagers, in good health, enjoying the life they were given. Steve and Angie exposed themselves in doing everything possible to save her babies, and avoid abortion, accepting the complex journey ahead of them. Long Process: Completing this event; bedrest began immediately and lasted fifteen weeks prior to being admitted to the hospital. Then nine weeks in the hospital before birthing her babies. Angy gained one hundred pounds, with minimal activity, for six months. Afterwords, Angie was in need of physical therapy to regain muscle tone, to return her ability to function normally, which took another nine months. Coming home, both Mary and Lindsey were in need of the best nutrition possible. They did not consume normal food for approximately three years, instead a gastric feeding tube system, placed in their abdomen, was used for that period of time. Between three and four years old, they began to adjust to oral intake, eating normal food and reacting to life under the loving nature of their parents.

Final Results :Steve and Angie have two surviving girls who bring complete purpose to their lives. They are grateful for their decision to continue this event under the power of God's will, enduring a burden, that has led to everlasting joy. Angie says; the girls are thriving in life, with little complications. School is really good for them, as they strive with others in their age group…who wouldn't even know how early they were born, or the adventure leading up to this point in their life. Mary and Lyndsey are now almost sixteen years old. Seeing them at church, coming to a youth group, I was surprised, Lyndsey drove to church using a drivers permit,: accompanied by her mother; then just recently came by herself having her own drivers license. Their outgoing personalities are infectious, it is a delight to know them. Lyndsey and

Mary have Blessed many, especially me. Bringing life into this world or aborting life, brings much controversy in understanding "why?" The sadness of aborting a child before birth as a form of birth control, without consideration for future life, and may result in lifelong guilt or remorse. Steve and Angie, considered potential death, and poor outcome, then decided to trust God in their commitment against abortion. They put their faith in God, to lead them to a good result.

Understanding Pre-Birth to Recovery: Most expecting Mother's seem elated to bring a new life into this world. The excitement of this process is fun. Uplifting comments from others., as their tummy grows in excitement. From a physical point of view, the first few weeks are not as bad as the last few days; when the moment of going through labor results in surprised discomfort. This is the turning point of all pregnant mothers… is when the fun part of pregnancy turns to the point of… **"Let's get this over with"!** Soon after the trauma of labor, is when they lay the baby into the mothers arms, as it crushes all pain into pleasure and love., as they look at this miracle of life!

Adopting a Child: The positive choice in an unwanted pregnancy, is to complete the process of birthing, then seek couples who want to adopt. In some cases, after the birthing process the mothers decide to keep their newborn. In other cases, the mother decides to find a couple that will give the best possible care to her child's future. My Son and his wife, decided to pursue open adoption. Unable to bare children, they soon adopted two amazing girls, from two thoughtful birthing mothers, who wanted the best for their child's life; rather than using available termination. Both of these mothers sought counsel and were able to choose the adoptive parents they wanted. Although they were not allowed to give input in raising the child, they were given the opportunity to have freedom to visit in the future. As the girls grew older, they wanted to meet their birth mother. The benefit of this choice is; the child has access to their birth parents, securing the knowledge of their natural history, as they all gather in the strength of family. Both girls have visited their birth parents, increasing a loving bond in all of us. Their presence is a gift from God to us, giving opportunity to love them as our own. Birthing your own child or adopting, makes no difference in the love of family.

Adopting a Child, with Severe Disability: Matt and Laura, are friends of mine who attended our church before moving to the Seattle area, from Spokane, Washington. Their history in finding each other; then marrying; is a story in itself, and will need another book to tell all they have done to… pay it forward! This remarkable couple have; two adopted children, two biological children, and two children from Laura's previous marriage, completing their family… or maybe not?

One day Laura was having lunch with the social worker,(who had arranged her two previous youngsters for adoption). During the conversation, the social worker talked about a young boy from Ethiopia, who is in an orphan devastated by a train accident…Loosing both legs and part of an arm, he had little hope to survive on his own, threatening to remain incarcerated the rest of his life. After hearing all that has happened to this child, Laura stated her condolences, and set aside prayer time to find good parents for his future.. As Laura headed for her car, she had conflicting thoughts in turning away from this situation. Trying to make peace… not committing to the challenge of adopting this broken life… she wondered if she should get involved or not? Calling her husband Matt, telling him the situation, she asked him what to do? Having a wonderful relationship, his loving response concluded that Laura could do what she thinks is best, and he would support her either way. Laura's life is unique and focused on paying it forward, meaning somewhere in her life someone helped her… so in gratitude she desires to do the same for others. She is guided by the grace of God, and is a true believer in His existence. Praying for Gods guidance, it seemed the only way to find peace, was to offer a commitment to save this innocent child from incarceration. Without influence of a cohesive family, this severely crippled child, (coming from a non-english speaking country, having no education, with dark skin, leading to possible disparagement, on his own without discipline, having possible anger issues, fearing what comes next, and is now in the fight for survival. Who, in their right mind, would want to commit to this radical undertaking of adoption? Laura is as beautiful on the outside as she is on the inside, but know this, she disregards her flesh, and concentrates on living a life by walking in the Spirit of God., along with her husband Matt. This remarkable couple were able to adopt and bring their new son 'Josh' home to America, when he was eleven years old.

Josh: Born in Ethiopia and lived with his father until he was seven years old. His parents were not married, and separated, so when his father died, he went to live with his Mom. After living with his mother and older brother, feeling unwanted; the pain of neglect from a mother and brother, drove Josh to leave their home and be on his own. At the age of eight, he had never been to school, he had no way to support himself, but left home and hitchhiked on a bus to Metehara, Ethiopia. Once there, he slept at Bus stops or any where else he could find shelter. Josh was not alone. On the streets of Ethiopia in 2003 there were many kids like him.; an estimated presence of 4.6 million Ethiopian children are missing one or both of their parents… some 800,000 of them are orphaned by the effects of HIV, AIDS. Josh doesn't know how his father died, because he left one day and never came back. While living on the streets, Josh made a new family, of kids like him. Kids without homes or shelter, or parents. Having to take care of themselves, when no one else would, or could. Bonding together, these kids became more secure in numbers, calling themselves 'Wolfpack', as Josh says. This group, composed of six kids, ranging from 6 to 14 years old, did not do crimes, but survived by gleaning from any the spoils they could find. Doing odd jobs as a team, sharing survival, staying in one place, reduced the opportunity to find food or work, they would also ride the trains to seek survival in other areas. Cargo trains were a valuable asset in hunting down items for survival in different areas. There were no rules for anyone who wanted a ride them, and many used the opportunity to do so. For the Wolfpack, short stops allowed them to jump off for a brief period to hunt and return, before the train started again. This is where his story gets interesting.

Josh tells his story: Josh lived several months in these conditions until the accident, which changed his life forever. Traveling from the Ethiopian capital of Addis Ababa to a city five hours away, the train stoped on schedule to deliver goods. This gave opportunity for the pack to jump off quickly scavenge for food and other items to use or sell. Josh says my pack got back to the train early, and I was still searching when the train started moving. Having no flatbeds available, I ran along side and reached out find a space between the cars. Preparing to jump, it seemed like I was pulled under, as the train accelerated, then every thing went black. When I woke up along the side of the tracks, I saw my right arm looking like a fresh green banana broken open, then I seemed to pass out again. Shortly, I woke up again to the sound of two people arguing. One said; let him die, he's almost dead anyway. Then the other person arguing said; No! You have to give him a chance! Almost being left for dead, I was taken to the hospital for care. The next thing I can remember was like a scene in a movie. A flash of brights flowing like a river over my head, as they rushed me along to emergency care. After that, I remember nothing else, until I woke up from a coma. Not knowing how long I had been there, it must have been a week or two, because, my aunt was at my bedside, and she lived in a village far enough away that it would be difficult to find. Also, two members of my Wolfpack found me at the hospital, then my mother had arrived as well. Mom chased the boy's away using an angry tone, and did not consider their circumstances, treating them like dogs. It didn't take long for me to remember what happened. I lost both of my legs and my right forearm was amputated, below the elbow. Physical pain was evident, but my biggest concern was my mother. As expected, my mother told the doctors she didn't know what she could do with me, indicating again, she didn't want me. So I figured I was headed to an orphanage for the rest of my life.

Treatment: Once hospitalized Josh was stabilized with surgery to his legs and arm. During recovery it was very painful for him because they did not leave room for proper healing and growth. After correcting this issue, the visiting surgeon Dr. Berry Hicks, took the young child home, to recover in Australia.. Hicks and His wife wanted to adopt him but they were unable to do so, because of the Ethiopian age limits of adoptive parents. So they returned him to an orphanage, in Ethiopia.. After doing this in agony, they made it their mission to find this young boy a suitable family.

Best News Ever: This is where our story gets better! As Laura listened to this case worker, then told me the contents of this meeting. Because she called Matt, I realized these amazing, true Christians, capture the essence of trusting the will of God. Praying for guidance, it seemed the only way to find peace, and offer a commitment to adopt Josh. Eventually, Laura and Matt were allowed to request adoption, requiring some time to spend in Ethiopia, to meet requirements, and bond with the child under their scrutiny. Laura accompanied with her teenaged daughter; were excited to make a place for this new member of their family. They endured the process of evaluation to be Family, hoping to assure his life did not go unnoticed.

Adjustment to the USA: Soon, Josh arrived at home, meeting Matt, and the rest of his new family. But, undertaking was not only a physical change, but also a new direction in a strange place. Josh was unaware of the life ahead of him, which created much anxiety and despair. Without the ability to speak english, this triple amputee, in a wheel chair, in a foreign country, had obvious trust issues, and struggled to accept his new family. Without foundation in education, he started the sixth grade, which elevated him to a level of learning without the experience of the previous five years. Unable to speak or understand english, his native language, Amharic, was useless. Another interesting point is, he was the only black person in the class. Coming from a nation of negro's, not understanding prejudice, that might add an additional burden in capturing a comfortable life. Out side of school, Josh also had to learn to speak english. At a special school of language, Josh says, it was the toughest thing I have ever done, Public School is no joke. Josh says, I didn't know it at the time, but for about three years being part of the family., over time, with much love and attention, Josh felt like he was home! My siblings love me and cared for me, and my parents supported me in everything I did, which broke down many walls.

My personal connection to Josh: I first met Josh when he came to our church with his family. I had no idea about his background, but wondered how the life of a triple amputee in a wheel chair wold turn out? Over the next few weeks it seemed he was overwhelmed with the challenges of his situation. One day at church, after setting up the doughnuts for refreshments, I noticed Josh sitting next to his mother (without his wheel chair), not having means to gather treats; I asked him if he wanted a doughnut? Before he could answer; Laura stopped her conversation; looking at me with her stern eyes… strongly remarking… if he wants a doughnut he will get up and get it himself! What? The sound of her voice surprised me. To think this wonderful Christian lady was being mean, I approached her away from this incident. Asking Laura what is going on? She explained Josh had prosthetic legs and refused to use them in favor of a wheel chair, which he has to depend on others to assist him into and out of the chair. It was not a big issue, but the ability to ambulate on his own, using prosthetics, was intended to show him a different way to life. The Wheel chair was finally approved. Eventually over time, everyone accepted in his choice to use the wheel chair, for his daily routines. This became a powerful link to improve his life to the fullest! Laura and Matt are not authoritarians, but more like negotiators with limits, always based on, "What would Jesus do?" Love, in spite of differences, is the key to a good negotiation, as the participants resolve issues satisfying everyone. However, at times, there may be a gridlock, removing understanding from the equation; a force of evil that torments everyone involved. It is sad, when prayer does not seem to be helping the tormented or lost, but many survive with concern and love, in spite of differences. Remember, God uses His good purpose to provide success or failure to all who believe, it is by His will we live.

A new beginning: While undergoing physical therapy at Shriner's Hospital for Children, Josh was approached by Teresa Skinner, an occupational therapist and executive director of the athletics organization, Para Sport. She suggested Basketball as a way for Josh to stay active. In Ethiopia soccer and track, are the most popular sports, and Josh knew nothing about basketball, however, he decided to try it. Josh says; I went out there and pushed a little bit and I was getting beat by everybody. Fortunately, it motivated me to continue in the program. From there on, it was like a way of meditation. Being stressed, or if I had too much going on in my life, I could overcome my anxiety, by being in the gym alone, practicing with my head phones on.

Success: Over time Josh fell in love with the sport. He spent six years playing: junior devision wheel chair basketball, while continuing to push himself in school. In 2015, His dedication to schoolwork paid off when he graduated from high school along side his best friends… the kids he first met in middle school. Graduating that same year, Josh's athletic ability paid off in a huge way. He earned an invitation to play with the US Wheel Chair Rugby team. Although he never played rugby he picked it up quickly and found himself competing at the 2016 Paralympics in Rio de Janeiro. The Team took home the silver metal, loosing to Australia by one point. Josh was among the Olympic and para Olympics, invited to the White House to meet the president and first lady. He shook Barack's hand and Michelle gave him a hug. Not even the President or his comrades in politics, can imagine what all these athletes have endured. To be in this situation, it takes much courage and hard work to overcome the demands of self-pity, while striving for self esteem. Accolades are common for their success; being motivated in spite of their disability. Nevertheless, they are among many others who do not receive the love and respect for their outstanding accomplishments in being handicapped. They illustrate, doing the best they can, accomplish tasks that lead to more independence, and a comfortable way Brewer was a member of the wheelchair rugby team in the 2016 Paralympic Games in Rio.

THE CHALLENGE OF CHANGE

Courage, determination and serenity, coming from GYM time.

Meeting the President of the United States, Far from his country it takes much courage and hard work to overcome the demands of self-pity, while striving for self esteem. Accolades for their success, being motivated, in spite of their disability, their silent battle does not go unnoticed among family and friends, who remind them of their uniqueness and successes, having deep love for them. Being around loved ones for an appropriate length of time, the actual handicap fades into the shadow of common ground, accepting the situation as what it is, bringing success to a potential future. Eventually, the spirit of the afflicted, is lifted, which may include humor and love spats, progressing to fun and games, accepting a valuable connection of spirit and self-esteem. After the success of representing the USA, Josh played two seasons for the Rough Valley Scorpions, a Division 1 wheelchair basketball team in Medford, Oregon. At this time he was setting a goal to play on the USA, Paralympic Basketball Team that has been one of his goals since he fell in love with this sport.

From Wolfpack to Wildcat: At the age of nineteen, he visited the University of Arizona campus and fell in love with the demeanor of the students. The Disability Resource Center, is home to the Adaptive Athletics Program, a major consideration that drew Josh to this University. Determined to attend the U of A, Josh moved to Tucson, to establish residency (a year earlier before he knew whether or not he would be accepted). Determined by the possibility of being a teammate, He work hard to perfect his game, wanting to be a member of the 14 player roster. Playing in a tournament in Houston, Josh received a notice by phone that he was accepted to the U of A, and placed as a member of the U of A Wheelchair Basket Ball Team. " I screamed, I really did; Josh said. This was the best thing I have ever heard! " With emotions of gratitude, joy and accomplishment, fulfilling his quest to reach the eventual goal of being on the USA Basketball Team, coach Derek Brown might be the one to help him accomplish his desire.

A Better Life: Josh, now at the age of twenty-two, lives off campus and shares an apartment with incoming teammates from Salt Lake City. He is as serious about academics, as he is all about basketball. When not training, he is hitting the books trying to soak up as much general knowledge as he can. The educational part of his life is an ongoing process, with hills to climb because of not being educated from the beginning. Not speaking the english language until the age of Eleven, he has gained ground, but now it is difficult to remember his natural language. With the struggle of education, Josh is the first of six adopted siblings to attend collage. He has nieces and nephews, and is close to his proud parents who live in Seattle, Washington.

Interesting Interaction: In an ironic twist of fate, his adoptive father, Matt, works in rail road maintenance. Surprised by the connection to the history of Josh, it gets an eye roll, or a good nature laugh in how Josh became a valuable member of this Family. Because of the rescue and determination to give him 'a chance', it appears that Josh has turned into a great example of what one can do with support, motivation and love. His motivation to turn a tragic loss into a powerful example of success, that appears to be a God send. From, those who seem to follow God's will, it motivates us to trust and serve in His counsel. The person at the accident site was speaking through Devine Intervention, when he said, " give him a chance! " That chance turned into an extreme example of what God can do through us! Interestingly, Josh has also heard from his biological mother, who found him on face book. Although he doesn't speak his native language, he uses google translation to communicate with her and his sister. Emotionally, Josh does not hold any negative thoughts. He hopes to visit his homeland in the future. Josh says; "It's been a tough journey, for me, one I will never regret or replace. I am thankful for every thing I have gone through". While there were plenty of moments Josh could have quit, … the driving force of survival and the focus of achieving goals, became his routine, leading to the new life he has and the faith that he follows. Josh has had the worst of the worst, knowing the threat of survival. He hopes to have the ability to "pay it forward," helping other people who do not have the means to support themselves, not just in the USA, but also Ethiopia. The streets I grew up on, the places I slept, the kids that nobody gives a lot of thought to; that's been on my heart. I have opportunity to do what I can, with what I have been given."

Writer Accolades

My thanks to Alexis Blue, The University of Arizona / Communications, for giving me excerpts from her, August 22, 2018 report, "Streets of Ethiopia to the USA," regarding the events in the life of Josh. Also, if you are interested in videos, in seeing Josh in action, Google: Josh Brewer Basketball Wheelchair.

Special Needs: Children born with special needs, set an example to all who know them. There are few parents who reject their situation, adjusting to doing everything possible to nurture and love, this new life. Some of those born with special needs, grasp their condition as normal, without thinking of what normal is. While I was in training, as a nurse, one study was responding to the handicapped. Choosing an impressive young female; born with cerebral palsy; in her early twenties; it was an eye opener to me. She remains independent, lives in her own apartment, and works for the Goodwill system, two blocks away. The advancement of her condition did not effect her ability to walk, but she struggles to put one foot in front of another, with an awkward gait. During the short time of befriending her, we went to dinner and visited her work place. She was well respected as a kind person, and a hard worker. At one point I asked her how she would feel without having her handicap? It was like I shot her in the chest, as she blurted out…I have no handicap… I have cerebral palsy. I do just fine! From then on I realized there are many who are handicapped, living life as normal as they can; proud of their accomplishments and ability to cope with their circumstances. However, the power of being compromised, handicapped or not, rests on the individual experiencing the condition. Some are often encouraged by family and friends. This surprising, confident, hard working woman, has given me a story to tell about the courage in being a unique individual.

Dinner with Sam: Ruben and Tammy are a remarkable couple who welcomed our church as a place to worship. Their presence and active attendance is a blessing to all that know them. The power of their remarkable adventure as a couple, is the deep faith they have in the God who created them. Married beyond three decades, having a total of nine children, their connection as a couple is expressed in the extraordinary faith they demonstrate toward, God; family; and future. By our request to befriend them, they invited us to dinner, to share their background with ours, and to get acquainted with their son 'Sam', who fits in the category of special needs. Sam, is nineteen years old. He was born with severe complications and diagnosed with downs syndrome. He is living in the innocent ability of a small child, unable to participate in normal conversations. A delight to be with, he interacts with others, revealing his playful personality. Sam is unlikely to progress, and will remain just as he is, until God Calls him home. Why is it, God challenges some to belong in the category of special needs, giving little ability in freedom to control themself independently? What is the opinion of others who are outside of this dilemma? Does opinion matter? Is it a pitiful situation? Or is it a test, or example of love and determination? God selects certain people, who have the ability to adjust, and use their love to serve, no matter what the issue. Ruben and Tammy are in that category. and in a way, are all special in God's sight! Many in this world, would not survive without getting help from others. The insecurity of 'why me' echoes self-petty and a selfish reaction at first, but most involved; find joy in this odd situation, by loving others.

This unique situation is challenging, but also exhilarating to those of us who have found love in this tremendous gift of life. Having a large Family or not, we all hope and look toward a positive event, as we bring new life into this world. Unfortunately, not all births are routine. .Sam had a complicated delivery in addition to being diagnosed with Downs Syndrome. Down syndrome: is a genetic disorder caused when abnormal cell division results in an extra full or partial copy of chromosome 21. This extra genetic material causes a developmental change and physical features of Down syndrome. Down syndrome varies in severity among individuals, causing lifelong intellectual disability and developmental delays. During dinner, we observed Sam and his playful attitude. I wondered what his demeanor was like when he got upset? Also how does his parents and family react to events in his daily life? What are the situations that require discipline and how is that accomplished? How does one find the endurance and patience to continue to care for a special need person? We must conclude that Sam, at the age of nineteen, is himself, without the ability grow any farther than his present circumstances. Like any young child, consideration is needed to have a continued safe environment and close observation for his safety. Adult supervision might be required at all times. These children with demeanor as a young child, can have high and low periods in their life, but with tender loving care or can be considered a valuable asset to family life. Sam is a reminder in the innocents of love. Unable to have strong knowledge, our wise opinions; he is a beacon to understand God is our maker, who allows innocence to prevail in all kinds of situations. The power of love exists in all of us, giving the opportunity to understand what it means to give and receive, when dealing with disability, or any other related need..

Disability, Substance Abuse and Death: Nick was Born August 28, 1991. Soon after birth it was discovered, Nick had a serious malformed heart. He was taken to Children's Hospital in Seattle, Washington, for evaluation. It was discovered surgical intervention was not possible at this time. He would have to be treated medically, but would eventually need surgery to sustain his life. For the next three years, his parents traveled to locations for expert intervention, providing the best of care possible. At the age of three, Nick was given an opportunity to transfer to UCLA for a cutting-edge operating procedure. This approach began a long road in keeping Nick alive and functioning. Through multiple surgeries, followed by physical therapy. Some success after having six surgeries by the age of six, and a few other corrective procedures, proved he was committed to living life with caution. Even in a safe loving environment, with a reasonable future, the burden of his adventures eventually took its toll on his psychological well being; effecting family, with an unwanted burden of self destruction. Blessed with caring and loving parents, adjustments to compensate for a child having multiple surgeries and recovery periods, leads to physical and mental exhaustion, as everyone seeks to find stability. Realistically, all children are special. Parents caring for children with special needs, seem to display understanding and acceptance to their role in caring for the ongoing process to stabilize life. They need to adjust their lives with endurance, compassion, and love, providing the best quality of life possible, under the circumstances.

In Nick's case, his family support could not have been better. All involved, yielded unselfish love in this delicate situation. His grandparents are like family to us, and although we did not get involved, our prayers were, and always are, with their family. Although his childhood was filled with medical intervention, Nick had some happy times growing up, and became a delight to those around him. Unfortunately, his early childhood, was often interrupted by hospital visits. Stressing his demeanor, took its toll on finding a comfortable way of life. He thrived as the family compensated to his needs, making him a central part of their lives.

When he reached puberty and adolescence, the strain of being physically compromised had a strong influence on the direction and decisions he made; while adjusting to his emotional and physical needs.

Not knowing the exact circumstances in Nicks adolescence, his time of life, was challenging as he tried to fit in with others. Even without the physical ability; teenage years alone can affect your life forever, with good or bad experiences.

Thinking of Nick, and remembering my difficulty as an outsider in high school, my view here is personal. How was your experience in high school? In Nick's case, I believe he was loved by many `. But being physically limited, as he watched others do what he couldn't do physically. This might have taken its toll on his emotions and common sense as he began to feel inferior. The feeling of being out side of the social norm; separated from the achievers, he began to seek others like him. My experience in high school was also out side of the social norm. But I did not seek anything, having few friends and my annoying older brothers. For me, paranoia begins in the hearts of those who already feel, they do not belong. Struggling with emotional pain can produce an unrealistic path toward the future. Thinking we are second rate, can lead us to launching a disaster; away from reality. Experiencing rejection, the inferior seek others, like them to remove the sadness that plagues their soul. As a teenager, the goal in learning social satisfaction, is to associate with others who are like-minded. In Nicks case, those who are in pain, seek others who are in pain, trying to find resolution to their needs. Social levels in high school can influence the direction of one's future. Most kids survive with a good experience, but some are not so lucky, left behind. with an inferiority complex. The unlucky ones might, come from a broken home. Often feeling the responsibility of causing a divorce; is a common culprit. Unable to cope with death is another; or illness in the family, or being poor, or any other events, can fuel low self-esteem, which creates a retraction away from the good in life; followed by an inferiority complex leading to the disaster of isolated living, I call 'outsiders'. They do not fit in the social population, falling in the shadows of decaying self worth and hopelessness. They are not evil, but many are misguided and unloved in society, because of their differences. Pain emerges to receive the label of being a societal menace. Abandoned by society, influenced by paranoia and anger, they bond together, then commit to their way of life, with destructive tendencies, having illogical views, being stubborn in their way of life, leading them to disaster.

They are lost, but somehow find comfort in knowing… they are not alone. They bond with others like them. Bonding with those who care about your problems, and share with you, seems to bring comfort and stability under the darkest of circumstances. Over time, they progresses to self-destructive conduct, leading to a world of abuse or violent outbursts. They seem to have no recollection of love, striking out at others; especially the ones who want help them out of this reckless, abusive, behavior!

Regrettably, Nick felt comfortable in this group: Which eventually led him to substance abuse and his demise. His grandparents are like family to us, and although we did not get involved, our prayers were and always are with their family. Their goal to guide Nick to a better behavior, they provided a place to live in a loving environment. However, the stress challenging Nick, to seek a more loving normal relationship, eventually failed. Over time, Nick was beyond comprehension. His action to lie, manipulate, steal and control his life style, consumed him to death. Nick died August 8, 2015, as he overdosed from substance abuse, just 20 days short of his 24th birthday. "I must be rigorously be honest with not only myself but others as well," was final comment before He died.

The Challenge Prior to his passing; Nick was attempting to change his ways, with much difficulty. Before his death, Nick wrote this final page in his journal. " I have felt, very motivated to change. I'm still scared, but I have a willingness now. For so long, I have felt like I have been swimming against a strong current, making no progress at all. Since I've come to the treatment, I have made great strides. It's almost as if I am in a marathon in my new life. I'm starting out strong and I'm making a steady pace so far, but I'm scared. I might slow down. I have always done the same things over and over. The only thing I have to change in my life is … everything! I want sobriety now more than ever. I must live my life day to day, moment to moment. I don't know what my future will hold, but I am eager to find out. I want more to life than just to exist… I want to live.!There is so much beauty in life, but yet I continue to look at the dim side of things. I like to avoid looking at my problems and focus on fixing those around me. Who am I to judge, he who needs to be fixed, when I can't even really look at myself? I must look into myself, to find the real me. I future will hold"… " I want more to life, than just exist"… "there is much beauty in life, but I look at the dim side of things"… "I can't judge others"…"I can't even look at myself "… " I often find myself playing life as if it is myself playing life as if is a game. I have played recklessly and carelessly. In no way would being like that, bring me victory. I must live life on life's terms. I will change, and I will make better goals. I must thank God every day, for every moment I get". When Nick's mother gave me this final statement from his journal, the sadness in his life was incredibly obvious: "I feel very motivated to change" … "I'm scared, swimming the current, making no progress"… " I have made great strides in coming to treatment, but It seems like a marathon"… "I'm starting out strong, but I'm scared I might slow down"…" I have done the same thing over and over"… "the only thing I have to change in my life is …everything"… " I want sobriety more than ever"… " I must live my life moment by moment…" I don't know what my a game"… " I have played recklessly and carelessly"…" I will change and make better goals"…" I must thank God every day, for every moment I get." The last comment in his journal is a striking example, allowing us to remember his birth, and consider the complex issue in his need to survive. Throughout his short lived life, because of those multiple surgeries as a child, the physical need for pain relief, solidified his desire to use it commonly; in difficult situations. Easily leading him to the psychological comfort found in addiction. Having little chance of turning away from its side effects, do to the dangerous pleasure it provides. Nick was loved by many, but during his emotional struggle and self value, he could not find a way to become normal. The seventeen statements above, are his gift to us. Presenting the core of low self esteem, leading to a personal battle that cannot be won, escaping to chemical abuse for comfort. How impossible it is to cure addiction, without early recognition and help! The death spiral of substance abuse takes its toll in emotional freedom., when dependent responsibility is lost, and self indulgence becomes the norm in life. Subjects who go down this path, must be identified early before it becomes a lifestyle out of control. Some think confinement is the best choice for withdrawal, because they are forced to become sober and think about their life. However, most of these individuals, have traded the challenges life, for physical escape; to avoid the pain of living in a situation of despair. Once bitten from the plague of substance abuse, it is not easy to regain self control. We all have a tendency to escape form hard times, by disregarding our troubles, in activities of pleasure. But, if we remain in control of our actions, we will soon understand our future depends on us, to compromise or find a solution to life's difficult demands.

In Nicks case, I can readily see his remorse in the path he took. From the beginning of his life, he was exposed to controlled substances during surgeries and recovery. It is obvious, the first six years of his life, gave him the desire to seek physical comfort, away from his pain and suffering. He made his life comfortable in joining a group of kids, that use the same high on drugs that he was given from all the surgeries he endured. An easy choice in the beginning, the entrapment of escape to physical pleasure, soon become suitable to irrational behavior. In his despair, Nick deliberately took his own life, overdosing from the substance he couldn't escape. His parting words…

"I must thank God, every day, for every moment I get." This statement makes me inclined, he was a believer. I am thankful for his honest and sincere last note in his journal, using it to help others understand; substance abuse, is a point of no return.

Terminal Disease: Marzell (Marcy) Grew up in a small town of eight hundred people, many locals in Troy Montana. A place where they were aquainted with each other, often demonstrating kindness, respect and concern for the well being of others. Marcy says; I didn't realize how much love was in this tiny town until my mother passed away and every church contributed to her funeral. Nourished by loving parents who believed in the 'Christen way of life'. Marcy attended church as a child. She says; I enjoyed that time when I was younger, but eventually became weary of the fundamentals of religion. In my late twenties, I tried to follow the ways of my parents by taking my children to church, hoping they may find peace in God. The guilt behind legalistic reasoning, or the pressure of pleasing my parents, influenced my faith and I turned away from the church with doubts. Providing for my family, a prayer at dinner, a sign of the cross, and a simple conversation, encompassed my new way of living without having to attend church.

Life for me was more recluse than outgoing and seems to be my comfort zone. I am not a woman of need, being independent, but I manage to give enough, and try to avoid taking anything at all. I chose marriage and family over the fundamentals of religion, avoiding the church, not understanding the true meaning behind God's existence, I soon pulled away from the routines of my parents, and guilt overcame my common sense.

Wrong Way: Substance abuse took control in my escape to find comfort, leaving me unaware of the death spiral I was in. Many who are caught in the trap of substance abuse think there is no way out from its stronghold, and in most cases that is true. But David, my boyfriend (now my husband) reached out to me and promised to help me regain my self-respect. Working in the tow truck business, we became good friends. However David wanted more. With my burden to alcohol and drugs, I did not want to be tied down in a serious relationship, so we dated for two years as free spirits until I got pregnant. At this point, with my condition, my immediate thought was to have an abortion. Fortunately, before this happened, I aborted naturally, now thanking God for removing yet another guilt trip in my life.

Today, we have been married twenty-six years, experiencing good times, as well as challenging times, remaining together as family. No matter what, I can truthfully say, David is my rock, who saved my life from disaster. We now have adult children and some grandchildren, who give us pleasure in our life, but over the years, there were difficult times. As empty nesters, the good and bad, never goes away between us, but our companionship is solid and our love is strong. Compromising and adjusting to conflicts, brings stability to our relationship.

In my late thirties, my mother was diagnosed with cancer. This single event became the lowest point in my existence. Words did not comfort, and reflections of our delightful life together, saddened every inch of my being, knowing our time together was limited. Having terminal cancer, Mom was in denial; "I am going to beat this thing and walk into heaven on my own", she said. Shocked by this reaction, knowing she lived 160 miles away from me, I drove home to be with her on weekends. For next eighteen months. I am grateful for the time I spent with her, learning more about cancer and the emotional challenges that involves all loved one's, friend and family. God took my mother home July 18, 2008.

In my family, our word defines our character. Religion by itself does not take mankind away from misdeeds and evil, but character and a man's word is essential in doing good business. My father and mother had the talent to restore antiques and make other items, often traveling to sell their merchandise in the surrounding areas. I also spent many hours in my Dad's shop learning and helping with the business. Falling in love with the process, was exciting, but having a steady income was not possible without making long term contracts. Eventually, the possibility of future income as a full vender, failed to meet our needs.

Soon after Mom... Dad had also developed cancer. After six surgeries and one with an infection, we took him Spokane, for a second opinion and care. However, we were too late and there was nothing left to do accept to keep him comfortable, and return home. In hind site, the larger community of Spokane, was much more progressive, and with early treatment, could have possibly saved my dad. The sadness of this situation, was not another low point in my life, but actually was one of elation. During his last days, Dad admitted to me, God was in your heart not in a church building. To me, loosing my Mom was the lowest point in my life, and my Dad's comment "God is in your heart, " changed my concerns about faith.

My Dad was always loving and important to me. My parents, surrounded themselves in the will of God, which lead me to research how to find God on my own.

I found comfort in attending a local church that teaches directly from the Bible. Calvary Chapel, just blocks away from my house, and teaches the Bible, verse by verse. This method, taking one book at a time, our Pastor rarely uses topical sermons, instead he applies application to what is being studied. As we progress, through the scriptures, verse by verse, book by book, I began to understand the power of reading the actual words, giving me opportunity to learn its content and apply it to my life. God's intent is to give us life beyond this existence, as we believe and trust in His Word. Individual prayer, and praying with others, understanding and acknowledging God's grace and mercy, leads to peace. Knowing we will eventually continue life in heaven, as Sprits. God's Grace is receiving the glory you don't deserve, and His mercy is not getting the judgement you do deserve from sin. This brings peace to your soul. We can not live this life without sinning on a daily basis. Anything that stands between you and God is sin. The power of the cross, believing in Jesus, makes us righteous in God's site, giving us opportunity to reconcile our sin, as Jesus sets us free from condemnation. Jesus has paid the price. He makes us free in God site. The simplicity of truly believing in the words from God, believing the value of what He has accomplished, in the sacrifice of his Son, we are now free from the punishment; headed to paradise as we follow in His ways. For many years, I have been wondering around life, trying to find what I didn't know I had lost. But now I know what I have gained in faith trusting the God of The Bible. My mother and father had an incredible love affair for each other, and faith in Jesus. My confusion about religion is now gone. I have finally found the reason to be in church fellowship, experiencing the power of the Bible. Being a like minded Christian, is like having an extended family to trust and rely on. What I've been missing all these years, came to me without question, without explanation, without judgment. My husband Dave and I have experienced the highs and lows of our relationship, but remain dedicated to each other, in spite of our differences. Adjusting to life one day at a time, living in the present, not dwelling in the past, but trusting God for our future, we are experiencing a good life in our middle age.

Then It Happened: At the age of forty-nine, like my Mom and Dad, dealing with cancer has now become personal. Three months before; I found a lump in my breast and thought it was hormonal. Now it's my turn… On May 16, 2019, I decided to see a doctor… it was cancer. My diagnosis was HER2 **positive**, meaning treatment could result in resolution. There are two categories defining treatment, the other is HER2 **negative**, leading to early demise, unable to resolve the condition.

The Plan: Learning about cancer by observing my parents death, I chose to be aggressive in the treatment. I elected to have a bilateral mastectomy 11/19 2019, followed by chemo treatment every six weeks for six rounds. In addition to adding Herceptin, to fight HER2 positive cancer. Herceptin is a monoclonal antibody, and it interferes with HER2. Using monoclonal antibodies to treat some types of cancer, either alongside chemotherapy or alone, cells produce proteins, and a monoclonal antibody recognizes and attaches itself to a particular protein. (Feb 25, 2019 Google). Receiving chemotherapy is not the most difficult part, nor are the surgeries. The most difficult part is shutting down my ability to be active in all things I love to do. I am lucky to have a chance to return to normal when this is over, all because of my family history, I made the right choice. Soon I will have reconstruction of my breasts, using my own fat from my stomach, like getting a tummy tuck and new breasts at one time. Grateful for a more natural look as I concentrate on remanning healthy,…but I'm still a work in progress. My Faith, in drawing nearer to my Creator, I hope to overcome the obstacles that keep me from befriending myself, in desire that all those I love, will be grateful to have known me.

Memo: How Many People Die of Cancer Each Year? In 2019, an estimated 606,880 people will die of cancer in the United States. Lung and bronchus cancer is responsible for the most deaths, with 142,670.

School Shooting: On September 13, 2017, a young shooter walked into a rural high School, then shot four students, killing one, injuring three, before being apprehended by a janitor. Joe B, rushed out of a bathroom in hot pursuit toward the sound of gunfire. Running in the hallway, directly toward the shooter, screaming profanities and threatening him to put the gun down! Surprisingly, in fear, the shooter dropped the weapon, seconds before he was apprehended by this life saving hero. Who held him by force until help arrived. The training Joe B. received in the military " fight or flight'" was reminder to run toward the enemy if it was possible to defeat them, or go the other direction and fight another day. The value in Joe's choice saved many injuries and lives, but in hindsight, the rush, without any weapon, might have gone another way. The value in this effort is to remind us that some threats are quickly resolved, while others last a long time. Some three hundred students were potential targets, located in the hallways, my friend Natalie was one of them who survived not being attacked. However her story, with her side kick Bella will mentioned in our next tragic event. In this radical mission to harm others, the shooter, just seventeen years old, was reacting to bulling and abuse toward him from others., however none who specifically offended him., were preset. The one student who died, was trying to stop his madness, by protecting others who were innocent. As he asked him not to do this .and was shot immediately. Killing one student. and shooting three others who survived, the emotional and physical scars of this event is mesmerizing. Today, four years later, the shooter is still pending trial. On January of this year 2022, at the age of twenty, the Court decided to charge him as an adult, with the possibility of life without parole.

Death and Extraordinary Injuries: Natalie (mentioned in the above school shooting) and Bella her best friend, graduated from High School 2021. Their enthusiasm, inspires all who know them. As best friends, they are molded together in sisterhood, having common goals preparing for the future. Celebrating their graduation this Spring, they took some time to relax and have fun, before returning to concentrated learning, in College. My Granddaughter Grace, is also a close friend and invited Natalie and Bella to her birthday party. Natalie and Bella decided to car pool and were always together, to enjoy some fun. After the party, while driving home, on a four lane highway, with a speed limit of 45 MPH; a driver in the oncoming lane, unexpectedly swerved across the highway crashing head on into their vehicle. Calculating the impact at about 100 MPH. The oncoming Driver was killed immediately, leaving the girls trapped in their car. They were totally unaware before this devastating impact. As the driver of their car; the crash left Natalie totally unconscious with massive injuries and Bella also injured, but remained conscious throughout the entire incident. Bella was the only one conscious at the scene, waiting for rescue, tormented in pain, emotionally aware of what just happened; retaining the moments after the crash. So Bella might be susceptible to possible psychological trauma in addition to being physical traumatized. During the recovery and aftermath of the accident, the shocking news was revealed, that both girls face a long recovery, lucky to be alive.

Graduation

The Unexpected Event

Grieving for these two girls began immediately and will carry on for some time .All who know them are praying, waiting for God to reveal the positive side of this tragic event. Considering the other driver died, with Natalie as the driver barely alive, Bella who remained conscious, scared and hurt, the dilemma of this shocking moment, will rest in the challenging future. Bella (red hair in photo), and Natalie (dark hair) will have weeks possibly months, or years, before returning to follow a routine schedule. The reaction from friends and family have been concerning. Some are angry, some are depressed or sorrowful, and some may blame God for harming these girls, but as believers in Jesus, they stand fast, knowing God will reveal His intent for their future.

It has been five months since the accident. Many are following the progress, and can see accomplishments but know this recovery will take time to stabilize their condition. The process of hope continues in all of us, knowing it is not over until it is over. Small steps of progress, with continued discomfort, mental and emotional grief, along with frustration.... that this is a slow process. Meanwhile their bubbly personalities offer fun and laughter as they progress to a more stable condition. With surgical intervention, and maintaining progress in daily routines, their delightful personalities and faith in God, is a message for all of us to follow.

As a nurse caring for intensive care patients, Bella was extremely lucky being on the passenger side of this accident, and avoid the extra trauma from the steering wheel and driving components that Natalie endured. However Bella's injuries were also threatening, and painful, in addition to remembering the accident, after impact. These two beautiful, intelligent young woman will be scarred for life as they struggle for recovery. The scars will remain, the trauma will be remembered, but most of all their spirits are intact, as they continue their journey to accept life as it unfolds. Using positive personalities, to approach. the future,. they are thankful for God's promise to bring them life in His kingdom, free from pain and suffering. Their story ignites hope in all who know them. Recently after burning their plastic back supports, (needed for stabilization) they can finally stand together and hope to get back to dancing. Bleaker's School of Dance. Owned by Melissa and Dion, have gifted our community by teaching dance, using the influence of the Christian Faith. These students are well trained in dance, starting from an early age of preschool, some even advance to college programs, and others as adults, to train new students in the school. Before the accident, there is a previous video showing Natalie and Bella dancing a duet, revealing how much their hard work has paid off. Their goal is to resume the joy of dancing again. Some who do not know them, will look at this accident as just another news story, some might even say a prayer, still others will be grateful it wasn't them.. But those of us who are intertwined with their lives, are saddened something like this would ever happen. These loving, sweet, reliable, innocent and responsible girls, are shinning lights too many. Why does this happen to believers in God, who have committed their lives to Him? The answer is found in His Word. God's love, grace and mercy, are presented as a gift to follow His lead, trusting His will, good or bad. It is essential to our faith, knowing God will never leave us or forsake us as we believe and follow His ways.

Proverbs 3:11-12 NKJ "My son, do not despise the chastening of the Lord, Nor detest His correction. For whom the Lord loves He corrects, just as a father of the son, in whom he delights." Chastening or not, God's will is sufficient for all who believe in Him. This life we live, is over quickly, offering many tragic events during its process. The afterlife of God's promise will prevail far above our doubts. Throughout the World, change effects many lives, some for the better or some for the worse, always pointing to the fact we are mortal and will eventually die!

Watching Natalie grow up, With her two brothers tagging behind, I have accumulated a deep love for this family. The passion they have in the presence of God, brightens the hearts of many, as they share their faith. Natalie's parents have been an essential part of our church. Amy, is the Children's Ministry Director, Don is a reliable confident servant to many, and also a system control agent during services. Their gift is to nurture kids to understand the love and promises; provided by our Creator. Amy has nurtured Natalie and Bella to be a leaders in children's worship, spreading the gospel. Their ability to guide others, children or adults, produces a guiding light to all who know them! Bella partnered with Natalie brings heavenly light to all who know them.

Recovery: Natalie does not remember the accident after impact, Bella remained conscious, remembering details of the drama while waiting for rescue. Bella, has a memory that may effect her or not. Counseling may be needed to allow closure to this event, in addition to her physical needs. But if you consider her personality after this event, their joyful presence continues as if nothing has changed. Both girls are lucky to be alive.. They remain close to those who are in their path, with concern and wellbeing for those in need. I am deeply proud of them, with much love and gratitude that God has put them in our life. For Bella and Natalie, crutches are used for now, soon to be gone. Focusing on life, nothing has changed; their uplifting spirits are ever present.

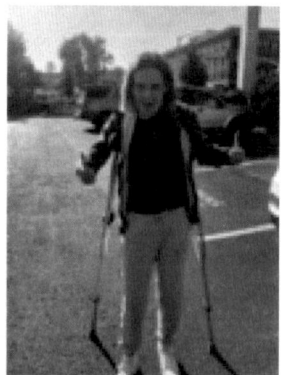

Today, Both Bella and Natalie remain sister close, as they move forward. Bella is almost recovered, and Natalie is still in the process of multiple procedures to correct the damage. Enduring the difficultly of multiple surgical interventions with a positive loving attitude. Why is this miracle of continued life brought to mind? Is God is using the strong, as an example to uplift those who need encouragement? Isn't His love for all mankind, found in the reward of giving everlasting life, without pain and suffering.? Whatever God is doing, rest assured, these girls are extending His love and presence, that others will consider faith in Jesus, and establish a unique place in Heaven where they are going.

Never Give Up on God: On September 25, 2009, Chuck, was waiting for a liver transplant. He spent the last two years hoping to extend his life. But after two years of waiting, he began deteriorating enough to place him on the critical need list.Not finding a donor to meet his need, at this point, it was suggested for him to get his affairs in order. Time was taking its toll on his possible transplant procedure, as his condition was deteriorating. They determined, about two more weeks of waiting, would be the end of having hope for the surgery. After two years, what is the chance of this happening, in just two weeks? Chuck says, after he returned home; every night I went to bed, I never knew if I would wake up the next morning. However, as one week passed and I was notified by the Hospital, they had a match for me! Excited when I got there, they prepared me for the surgery and were soon ready to complete the task. After being sedated, not knowing what was going on, I soon learned the donated liver was not suitable for transplant, when I woke up from the anesthesia, I was devastated to find, the surgery was canceled. Being excited in the beginning, my elation turned to despair. In just a few hours… I was going home to eventually die!

Turning to God in prayer: Seemed to be the only option. As they prepared to transport me to the exit, I began to Pray; "Dear Lord it seems like these are my last days and there is nothing I can do to change my situation. I am being sent home without the procedure. Now, Lord if it is your will… what ever your plan is for me, I am giving all of my hopes and dreams to You, right now. Please dear Lord, be with me! Give me a sign that You are real, and hear my prayer." Surprisingly, just before being discharged, Chuck's prayer was answered.! Remarkably a patient had passed away, having donated his remains, the surgeon concurred his liver was a solid match. Now, not leaving, but headed for the transplant, Chuck's miraculous prayer, received God's response, noted not as a fairy tale; but as a truthful, remarkable, answer to prayer.

Chuck says; this incident occurred on September 25, 2009 (my Dads Birthday). This is a day I now claim 're-birth in a gift from God.'; who gave me extended life, to be with family, knowing I will eventually receive ever lasting life in heaven, when my flesh is gone. Truly believing my spirit is alive forever, Jesus is my savior, the Holy spirit is my guide, and the powerful life our loving Father has given us, it is my hope this story will benefit others to give thanks to God for His mercy and guidance for all who believe in His loving Grace, kindness and forever promise

This short story is a huge example of how God works. We never know His will, because it is central to us, so we pray to concur, His will is our guiding hope. Chuck left a message in prayer, and understood the will of God is final. His love for us is always faithful, in every situation. Even sacrificing His Son on the cross, for the propitiation of our sin. Jesus has removed all of our sin forever. By believing, Chuck's prayer, indicates it is God's will only. As we communicate and trust, He is always faithful, in His choice, for our benefit.

THE GRAPE FROM GOD:

CHAPTER THREE

Poem: "I was nothing, then I am. A seedling to be planted, nurtured to grow, watered and fed waiting to be, a beautiful fruit, pleasing to see. Learning to know you as I remain, feeling the blessing of the sun and the rain. Life can be wonderful, or sad at times, being young, or growing old. Now I am wrinkled meeting your goal, pleasing the maker of my soul. Knowing the power of Your creation, I once was a grape, but now I am a raisin." (Ed Conine 2014)

As a Fruit: the grape has no choice but to accept its fate. There is **no compromise or** change, because the intention is; to produce nourishment for the living. Unlike the grape: God has given us a brain, filling us with everything we need to survive and grow. He not only provides food and shelter, but also gives us an opportunity to know Him, as our Creator. God loves us as His highest created beings, giving us a reason to reach out to Him for Help, not by demand, but by free will, understanding the power of His love is by His will only! Love is a strong word that demands a lot from all of us. As we use words to express our feelings for one another, the hope of having a relationship, is intended to acknowledge a good friendship. Being able to love one another, is God's intent for us. That said; making friends would be easy if we can maintain a comfortable interaction over time. However human conduct, as the Bible says… is weak in the flesh. To maintain a good relationship, it is a process of 'give and take', using your abilities to maintain stability. In a relationship, with compromise, and understanding we view one another's opinions, attempting mutual ground, to interact with one another, toward peace. By choice we can use the power of God's love, to build a good friendships, even when we have different opinions.

I am grateful for, the joy God has bestowed on me, as I completely yield my soul to Him. Attempting to follow His ways as best I can, using the power of His word, convinced of His presence as my guide, the essence of my faith is uplifted When I pray, it comforts me to truly believe He exists, and is willing to live with me forever in His Kingdom. The contract I make with God enlightens my soul, He will never forsake us, as we trust in His Will and follow His ways. The Bible teaches us to believe in Jesus as our lord and savior and live forever in Heaven. If we believe that truth, why not apply it to our worldly living?

Divorce and Abandonment: Why is it, finding love and long term companionship seems to be deteriorating in our society.? Growing up in the forties and fifties, the norm was to help your neighbor when needed, and also love and protect your family. As you think of this, keep in mind our worldly troubles began to rise because of 'abandonment and divorce'. In the forties, our society, shunned living together without being married. There might have been many living together, without being married, but it was kept a secrete from society. Today it is an open book, claiming free will, as the choice for many, which is not completely trustworthy to anyone.

Divorce is the enemy of common ground. The vows of marriage seems to be obsolete. My Mom and Dad, stayed together all of their married life, dealing with difficulties, but always supporting their marriage and family.. However the pressures having having poor income, and raising three scrappy boys;`turned them into alcoholics….but they kept the sanctity of family bonding, and marriage until their death, knowing Jesus our Savior.

My older brother died at the age of thirty-nine, he was divorced three times and having another marriage pending at his death. His problem was physically having a bad heart, being a compromised candidate for a solid marriage. However he had a loving soul, but his wild side overcame his common sense.

My second brother was forced to get married, having twin girls out of wedlock, Then eventually having third child, before their marriage ended in divorce. Then he married once again to the love of his life, who eventually divorced 'him', due to his lack of maturity, and stubbornness. Once more, he added a third wife, who manipulated him for financial gain. After divorcing his third wife, he remained single until his death at the age of 81. Without a wife, his kids loved and cared for him to his last days. My question is:, What happened to being married until death do us part?

Fore me as the younger brother, my marriage began with "eloping to be together in secret." However, eventually our secret became known, and we were re-married in the Church, revealing our faith in God. The surprise to our story, is; on October 4, 2023, we will celebrate our sixtieth year of marriage.

The sanctified part of marriage is to stay together, and work for resolutions leading to tolerance, trust, forgiveness and reconciliation, with a servants heart. In our early years of marriage, we had some dramatic exchanges. and we decided to seek counseling…(mostly for me to get a grip on maturity). Why is it, marriages separate, rather than use their intelligence to find compromised satisfaction? Most separate and divorce without recollecting their commitment to love; leaving scars in many families, without attempting to resolve negative issues. Mutual agreement is difficult because it is common for one person to dominate the other, conforming to their way of life, seldom considering to the opinion, of the other. The sweetness in finding someone to love for life, can be complicated if one is set in their ways., without compromise or understanding. I am thankful we survived our differences, but it is notable, that today's society, is fading away from what God intends for us. This topic, might reveal the worst change in all of us. Human conduct of concern and truth, is fading away into opinions of disagreement, lies and evil, rather than seeking resolution. It is amazing how many people are solidified in having their way, without consideration of compromise or acceptance to others So how come I didn't get divorced? It was a close call, but my loving wife had stamina and pity on me, to grow up and be a man! Still questioning if I made it to manhood, I realize God has sent me an Angel to guide me in the process of maturity.

Disability and Old Age: Disability is a challenge adjusting to life as it is… old age is a disability, challenging to the end of life, as it is… Both situations present a need to find stability, and satisfaction with endurance and compromise.

These two categories seem to fit just about everyone on this planet. No matter what, born with a handicap, or obtaining one during your lifetime, is inevitable at any age. Accepting change, the best existence possible to ongoing progress. Using facts, is the beginning of recovery to approach a change knowing what you have, and understanding to what you need. Part of the resolution, is leaving behind any loss that will not come back. Testing our abilities are common, as we approach a verity of change in our daily life. Many challenges are easily recognized, often resolved in similarities of the past, or by having easy access to a comfortable resolution. However, those of us who are exposed to a surprising or dramatic change, away from the norm, are specifically challenged to achieve balance toward a different way of living. The burden of physical or mental conditions altering our independence, will commit us to resolve things we face in our lifetime. Understanding what you can do, or cannot do, is a good place to begin. Some situations will test your ability to fight, or concede to the problem at hand.

Disabled or Old, we must to find common ground to redirect our life, avoiding the agony of change we cannot control. Moving toward a reasonable way of living, with new adjustments is not easy. Focusing on the positive instead of the negative is one way of keeping anxiety at bay. The of battle self-pity is the first thing to overcome. If you consider others who have greater problems than you, be grateful you are not one of them. Self-pity will override activities discouraging to your self-worth. It is essential to understand your condition and except your fate. Then find the strength to control what you can, to maintain control in pain and suffering, to the best of your abilities. Pain and suffering is easily identified in the act of growing older. In the age of geriatrics, you can be assured mental and physical problems will take its toll on your well being. Seeking self-esteem, to a more productive approach, using positive accomplishments to override the negative… is a good plan. ` But also remember, physical discomfort and loss of common abilities will effect your will to adjust to the circumstances.. There are many disabled who are unable to maintain daily routines. Without help, they may loose their ability to thrive. Interaction by caretakers, definitely occurs in the aging. The need to lift respect and self esteem, maintaining a relationship of common goals is critical, sharing or telling stories, and including others to participate, is the best way to lift spirits. Attending church may not be good for some, but spiritually and physically, it is the best activity to experience how to love others with concern and kindness. Disabled or old, there are some living a devastating experience, often impeding hope toward a stable life.

The Bible is the most encouraging book to find answers toward many problems.

Ecclesiastes 9:10 NKJ " Whatever your hand finds to do, do it with your might; for there is no work or device or knowledge or wisdom in the grave where you are going." -**2 Corinthians 4: 16-18 NKJ** " Therefore we do not lose heart. Even though our outward man is perishing, yet the inward man is being renewed day by day. For our light affliction, which is but for a moment, is working for us a far more exceeding and eternal weight in glory, while we do not look at the things which are seen, but at the things which are not seen. For the things which are seen are temporary, but the things which are not seen, are eternal. "

Review: Reviewing my life, it is incredible to discover the spirit within me. God explains the value of our living spirit is eternal, while our flesh is eventually headed for demise. The power of God's love is found in His word, the Bible; blessing all who believe and follow. As the aging process of life continues. the fear of death is a common. Looking at the mirror, reveals the aftermath in the progress of time. The flesh we live in… is fading away, soon to be forgotten in favor of the living. There are many times we might think, why doesn't God take us home quickly without suffering or discomfort? What is the purpose or need to be in difficult situations, especially for long periods of time? A reminder for me is to think of things that are not seen. Believing my spirit exists, bonding to God's promise (His Love), wanting us to join Him forever, in His Kingdom, helps me relax and endure whatever life produces. However, hard times still make me whine, cry and pray a lot! Experiencing pain, doing things as in the past, now challenges a new approach to normal chores. Morning brings a routine of things to do, but function and ability toward physical activity, makes it a contest to get things done. Hopping out of bed, rushing into anything that requires physical demand, is futile. During the past couple of winters, I enjoyed the process of writing this book, thinking my sedentary activity is a blessing, away from physical demands. Now it is spring, my yard work is limited, and the weeds continue to grow. In the past, excited to care for all that is needed, usually did not take much time, and the reward is wonderful. Now, unable to keep a moderate pace, my shop time has been reduced to two or three hours depending on endurance and pain. Also the yard work is an extreme challenge. The reality of my condition is evident, as I recognize my abilities are dwindling into a sedentary adjustment of old age. Do to weakness. I truly believe the aging process; is God's way for a final call; reminding us, our eventual physical demise is drawing near. An opportunity for us to reflect on the past, easily allows us to remember simpler times, compared to the present. Being active is important to everyone. The challenge for many aging Saints is to discover normal activity… is not guaranteed. We all hope to be comfortable in our daily routines, however, the aging process presents the inevitable, as we adjust to a slower pace… hoping the hitches in our get-a-long will allow us the opportunity thrive at family events. Sometimes uncomfortable physical demands are the issue, but most of all, the slowing of our brain and having a few spastic moves, can lead us in a path of clean up, like the food treats on our shirt, for example. The loss of coordination, allows us to exercise coverup, as we try to hide the evidence of our misfortune. Another challenge of old age, is keeping sane. Feeling many body parts beginning to fail, the issue of discomfort and pain captures your attention. Trying to avoid discomfort, our pathway leads us to maintain what we have, or face the consequences of deterioration and geriatric paranoia., as we struggle for stability. Gazing in the bathroom mirror, will eventually become your enemy, as you glance at your image… thinking a prune is not a bad fruit. Sometimes, making faces, and thinking is this someone else? You reluctantly concur the old one in the mirror is still you! However, our flesh is nothing, when compared to our spirt living inside of us. The flesh will pass away, but our spirit will live on, as we change to the likes of Jesus.

Approaching eighty: In a one year, **I often wonder** if the waddle hanging from my chin will end up being a bow-tie.? Also, the secrets found in my body habits, seem to becoming more public.! Gathering around people in the grocery store, some seem to think I need help (and I do), but I never let them know it. Having a pleasant attitude, is a key to satisfaction. Sharing the challenge of aging, can send us in a spiral of despair, if we do not stay focused on the here and now. Humor is a wonderful way of laughing at this predicament. Visit a nursing home, then try to find someone using their positive energy… it will melt your heart! You know you're getting older when you have two parts of a brain, ('left' and 'right'. In the left side, there is nothing right. on the right side, there is nothing left. The good in growing older, is having many pleasant memories, the bad is, you can't recall any of them? The little old gray haired lady you just helped across the street, is your wife. Your mind worked well in the beginning, getting to the bottom things, but now your bottom is having an affair with your favorite recliner. When you bend over to pic something up, you look for anything else while you are down there. You notice your body is making the same noises as your coffeemaker. Everything hurts, and what doesn't hurt, doesn't work. You think you still got it, but nobody wants to see it. Do not think of it as getting hot flashes, it could be your inner child playing with matches. You know how to prevent sagging, just eat until the wrinkles fill out, or hang upside down like a Bat, when sleeping. You have too much room in the house, and not enough room in the medicine cabinet. You look forward to a dull evening. Your mind makes contracts, your body can't keep. You finally reach the top of the ladder, but find it leaning against the wrong wall. Reaching retirement is a dream of when? Experiencing retirement is a question of, what now?

Disability is also in the "what now" category. "What I do as a man, is judged by the law of the land. What I do in spirit is judged by God." Both man and spirit belong to God, and cannot be separated or judged by anyone else. According to the Bible, those who do not believe in God, are lost. But f you do believe God exists, then search His word, and recognize the gift of His Son; Jesus who is the power of our salvation! Giving eternal life, by believing He is, who He says He is, presented as both God and man. Sincerely believing in the name of Jesus, with love, you will know God is love. If you don't have love, you do not know God, and will die. Developing my routines in old age, dealing with some tasks, that are physically uncomfortable, is routine. Doing the task or not, pain and discomfort, seem to override my ability to focus on physical actions at hand. I try to be useful, but the dilemma of the aging process with pain; threatens my abilities to function. Pain threatens my common sense, and sometimes leads to disorientation, or anger.

Breakfast before work, at the age of 20.

My portrait, presented by my wife and daughter, trying to figure out how I came to look like this, at 79. Some proclaim a picture says a thousand words, why is that? Everyone can relate to life, living through physical change, not realizing the eventual process of aging. Taking thought to visual presentations over time is normal. Staying away from reflections, gives us the opportunity to believe we have we have not changed much . Eventually, there comes a moment we would like to go back to when we looked our best, capturing that image forever. But that is not possible. Experiencing deterioration in the aging process, concentrating on the need for pleasantness, directs me to enjoy the time I have left… with whatever I have left!

Why did God give us joy of laughter? What benefit does humor play in our lives? What kind of joy do we get from saying or doing silly things? What are the things that make you laugh? What is the difference of being comical or obnoxious? When telling someone an amusing story, how does it feel to be part of their laughter? Have you ever tried to use humor to lift the spirits of one who is troubled? How does it feel when the effect of your humor is not working? How does it feel if your humor is offensive? What is the reward when succeeding to lift the spirit of one who is oppressed?

Working as a nurse, one characteristic in my life, is to use humorous quips to check the demeanor of my patients and their family. Using this approach in a hospital setting is a benefit for me, to recognize the emotional status of patients, and family. Although my listening skills need improvement, I find humor builds a closer interaction. Laughter is good medicine. Diversion in time of distress, humor is a welcomed event, to sublimate suffering, in hope for a better future.

Grieving: My best friend and I shared the ups and downs of our lives together, with honesty and truth (except for some little white lies). Bonding in comfort, benefited us in finding peace behind stressful situations. With true hearts, attempting to find stability, sometimes one had to alter the situation to find temporary comfort, considering the challenge ahead. On Christmas Day, 12. 25 2013, Dennis Kent Waltermire suddenly past away. We bonded together over fifty years as friends. Having met in the military, Denny was truly my brother from a different mother. One of our favorite interactions to each other, is the question; Are you just being stupid? Or are you being a stupid Dummy? Noting that stupid dummy was the lowest level of stupidity one could get. Denny's presence is gone, but His spirit is intact. We will meet again in Heaven, still laughing at this personal quip. Fortunately we both found a true belief in the God of the Bible. .Our youthful playtime, had mostly ended, helping us to be more discrete in our actions, by being connected to God. We certainly made use of reconciling our sinful ways, as we committed to faith in God, we truly believe there is life after death, and Jesus is the center of it all!

Thinking of Retirement: My wife and I had no plans in what to do next? However, we did cherish freedom away from the workforce. Before retirement, we experienced physical health issues possibly challenging our hope for the future. At the age of 54, diagnosed with cancer, I was able to have surgery to prolong my life. My friend and pastor Jerry Horgan, a Jew, and educator claiming Jesus Christ, also discovered cancer at the same time. However he did not survive more than one year, because it was inoperable. Jerry and Ken Parker are two pastors who encouraged me in a better understanding of the Bible. However my Son David, has been my teacher for the past 25 years; helping me build my faith in the truth of God's love. Understanding His loving will, He wants everyone to recognize the gift of everlasting life; found; as we believe in Jesus.

Early Retirement: At the age of 59, my wife Pam, lost her hearing in one ear and had to leave her position as an operating room nurse specialist. As a teacher, manager and confidante. Her impairment hindered her ability to hear background requests, while monitoring incoming calls. It also effected her ability to determine the direction of sound. Hearing aids did not prove to be effective. The best treatment was to to have an implant placed, to improve sound. Although it was successful, some conversations remain difficult to comprehend, and moderate noises threatened her hearing ability.

Pam was more than the average nurse, concerned with the best possible outcome of all procedures in the operating room. She was chosen to attend the new laser presentation in California, with surgeons, educating the fundamentals of using the new product approved. for use. She was the only nurse reviewing this procedure. Also, while I was

THE CHALLENGE OF CHANGE

in the Air Force, Cheyenne, Wyoming, she managed both surgical and recovery rooms, at the local hospital until we transferred to Travis Air Force Base, four yers later. Because of her current hearing loss, Pams early medical retirement became very emotional. Then God gave us the opportunity to rescue her parents, two hundred miles away. The awareness of Pam's hearing problems soon faded, as we were able to place a manufactured home on our property assuring care for her parents, to end of their life. God demonstrated his love and power, exposing His love, in this situation. This event was a Blessing!. Allowing Pam to be free from the work force, gave us the opportunity to care for her aging parents, full time! Thank God, for His loving kindness, making us comfortable in this situation., as we cherished our final moments together.

In my retirement, after having a knee replaced, then a complicated back surgery, the awareness of old age became evident to me. Adjusting too mild and moderate, discomfort seems to be the norm in old age. Evaluating my abilities to accomplish daily tasks, revealed an unexpected slowness in achieving my goals. My wife, also, after having a knee replacement, and other issues, acknowledged commitment, to her new lifestyle. It appears, regular tuneups and replacement parts are not uncommon in the elderly experience. The ability to remain active and functional, is our hope and goal for the rest of our life. However, the aging process effects our ability to build stamina.. Trying to survive as best we can, we grow weaker as time moves on. Our comfort zone is a constant reminder, in the struggle to remain normal. It is evident. that sometimes our ability to remain peaceful, is challenged by the degree of discomfort, we try to suppress. Emotionally we are at risk, knowing the effort of exercise will not produce a healthy comeback, and could even interrupt our status quo! It is not surprising that conversations with our peers are based on how to maintain, keep, or endure, our physical well being. Unlike dying quickly, the process in accepting old age, is to avoid what you cannot do, then work with what you can do. Having, self-esteem is important to maintain confidence. Being loved by the mix of family and friends, motivates finding a way to keep active. It tests the purpose to your existence, bringing value to those around you. Realizing you are in the outer perimeter of family inactivity, can bring a feeling of isolation. However, if your family history provides many gems in the bondage of love; it produces much gratitude by revealing you're past experiences. Physical changes in the old age are obvious. The results of an aging body, combines a verity of physical discomforts, often consuming our attention to be in the mix of daily life. Continual efforts to be active, may soon develop into being recluse. The power of our spirit, exemplifies our opportunity to acknowledge our condition, then proceed as best we can, without giving up.

Imitating Christ's Humility: Philippians 2:1-5 NIV "Therefore if you have any encouragement from being united with Christ, if any comfort from his love, if any common sharing in the Spirit, if any tenderness and compassion, then make my joy complete by being like-minded, having the same love, being one in spirit and of one mind. Do nothing out of selfish ambition or vain conceit. Rather, in and humility, value others above yourselves, do not look to your own interests, but each of you to the interests of others. In your relationships with one another, have the same mindset as Christ Jesus."

This scripture reminds me to serve others as best I can, if not physically, then using the power of prayer, is a sufficient enough to help others. Physical abilities are of value, but the capacity to share with others, easily overrides physical strength. Not being alone, brings value the presence of God Himself. He is always listening, waiting to communicate with those who love Him. Another uplifting moment, is the use of memory. Pleasant memories of my parents, my family, and friends, from past times, illuminates my soul. Remembering many powerful moments, reflecting much love of treasured times, detours emotions to a more comfortable topic.

My Private Place: A long time ago I questioned if I close my eyes…what do I see besides my eyelids? What do I hear in the sounds around me? What is going on with my physical presence? As I close my eyes, in memory or thought, my head tilts back as if I am looking up for an image to appear. Then I identify, it is just me, looking at my eyelids, in my secret place of thought, where no other will know what I am doing… accept God; (unless I decide to share openly with others.) There is something special about closing my eyes for a period of time. But on average, most people blink around 15 to 20 times each minute. That means, while you're awake, you probably blink; 900 – 1,200 times an hour; 14,400 – 19,200 times a day; 100,800 – 134,400 times a week; between 5.2 and 7.1 million times a year,… is this something to be aware of? Blinking will: Clear debris from your eyes, like small particles from the air, dried tears, and dead cells. Bring nutrients and other substances to your eyes that help keep them healthy. Wetting your eyes, which prevents Dry eyes and reduces your risk of problems with your tear film, bringing oxygen to your eyes. All of the above functions help prevent eye infections. Additionally, blinking lets your brain briefly rest, helping you refocus on whatever it is you're doing. When you rest your eyes, using your eyelid as a cover, you essentially tell your body to relax and take a break from focusing or thinking. Dr. Chiara Cirelli, explains; "while we're awake, all of our neurons are constantly firing, but that when we're asleep, the neurons revert to an 'up-and-down' state in which only some are active at a given time. During some stages of sleep, all neuron activity goes silent." As you rest your eyes, the neurons will never go completely silent, but they do actually take a break and reduce stress. A new study suggests that closing one's eyes in thought, actually does help an individual recall things in more accurate detail. Closing one's eyes will "help people visualize the details of the event they are trying to remember. (Dr. Chiara Cirelli: a neuroscientist; University of Wisconsin.)

Prayer: Nothing can invade this personal, isolated space, representing our personal feelings and secrets; except interruption from the outside world. It is interesting to note the above example is very like the power of prayer. If we use our minds to protect our privacy, we can also use these moments of silence, to commune with and befriend God; who knows everything about us.

Open prayer: is not the same as private prayer, because our private secrets remain directly in God's judgement alone. Meditation is a fantastic way to clear your mind and sometimes escape reality, to make the mind calm and peaceful. Reading the Bible, God's word claims… 'meditate on these things !

Definition of prayer: noun: A solemn request for help or expression of thanks, addressed to God or an object of worship. 'I'll say a prayer for him', or let us pray now; demonstrates a life of conviction through prayer leading to God Himself. Prayers, are the power in all religious service, especially the ones that gather in unity, serving the God of the Bible, as best they can.

Heaven: Uncertain of what is beyond this life? Many who are no longer with us, are separated from our loving God for eternity. All because they refuse to know Him. Seeing is believing! So it must be a big surprise to those who come before God, after death, for the first time in Heaven; shocked by His presence, destined by His judgement… All because they turned away from the choice to know Him, or not.

Choice or No Choice: We don't train to earn salvation. Rather, just the opposite: As we realize how truly wondrous our salvation is, it reshapes our priorities, our perspective, and the very things we live

for as each of us faithfully runs our own race of faith in God's strength.
By Adam R. Holtz, Our Daily Bread

Among the many changes we face each day, the most difficult is adjusting to alternatives in physical and emotional well being. Common illnesses are tolerable, because we are confident they will pass, in a short period of time. However, there are other situations that may challenge your life forever. Overcoming or adjusting to these events are critical. Success will depend on how you adjust to a different way of compromised living. Unwanted change increases our anxiety and fear. Why? Because we did not plan for it. Our demeanor is to pursue happiness. Unexpected change, is not considered until it happens. Without previous planning or direction, the individual participants find themselves in a dilemma of how to rekindle stability. Our ability to adapt to changing events, rests on us, as individuals. Life is personal. Adjustments must be made to our satisfaction, as we seek a new goal to regain comfort and stability. Sadly there are many who give up their fight for a suitable compromise, in favor substance abuse, reclusion, or suicide; by avoiding positive things they are not capable of controlling. It is up to us to choose our future, no matter what happens next. Compromising situations are common in everyday life. Most are easily resolved choosing between several options. However with abrupt physical/mental change, options are limited in adjustment and time, and produces a prolonged period of anxiety, until motivation and acceptance is concurred.

Encouragement from Jesus: 2 Corinthians 1:3-5 NKJ : "Blessed be the God and Father of our Lord Jesus Christ, the Father of mercies and God of all comfort, who comforts us in all our tribulation, that we may be able to comfort those who are in any trouble, with the same comfort which we ourselves are comforted by God. For as the sufferings of Christ abound in us, so our consolation also abounds, through Christ".

Faith prevails in all changes: Matthew 6:25 NKJ: "Look at the birds in the air; they do not sow or reap or store away in barns, and yet your heavenly Father feeds them. Are you not much more valuable than they?" Do not look back to what was… look forward to what is! Adjust to daily events, press forward to what you can do, rather than dwell on what you cannot do. Accept your limits, and gain confidence in your abilities of progress. Understand; life is short and some of those experiencing unwanted or prolonged change, need to find peace in their situation.

Matthew 6:26-33 NKJ " Therefore do not worry, saying, 'What shall we eat?' or 'What shall we drink?' or 'What shall we wear?' For after all these things the Gentiles seek. For your heavenly Father knows that you need all these things. But seek first the kingdom of God and His righteousness, and all these things shall be added to you.". If God cares for the non human life in His Creation, He will also look after us, as His child, to stay close to His lead and remember, by faith, you will prevail.

Hope: The God of the Bible is Hope and Truth to all that believe in His existence. Gathering many in prayer with cohesive intent, or individually seeking to understand God's will, is the basis for our communion with Him.

| Matthew 6:8-13 NKJ | Luke 11:1-4 NKJ |

The Lord's Prayer

There are two accounts are found in the new Testament:

Matthew 6:8-13 (the words of Jesus himself, interpreted by many): "Therefore do not be like them. For your Father knows the things you have need, before you ask Him." In this manner, therefore pray: "Our Father in heaven, Hallowed be Your name. Your kingdom come, Your will be done, On earth as it is in heaven, Give us this day our daily bread, And forgive us our debts, As we forgive our debtors. And do not lead us into temptation, But deliver us from the evil one. For Yours is the kingdom and the power and the glory forever, Amen."

Luke: 11:1-4 NKJ " One day Jesus was praying in a certain place. When he finished, one of his disciples said to him, Lord, teach us to pray, just as John taught his disciples. He said to them, When you pray, say:"'Father, hallowed be your name, your kingdom come. Give us each day our daily bread. Forgive us our sins, for we also forgive everyone who sins against us. And lead us not into temptation

Matthew 6:8-13 NJK Is spoken by Jesus himself and is the traditional accepted version coming from God Himself. As we close our eyes to pray this prayer, focusing on the words of an invisible Creator who is speaking in the flesh, it is important to follow Jesus in this presentation. Many times in my life I have repeated these words rhetorically, eventually finding myself saying the words, without glorifying the power of what it represents. This personal moment in prayer is intended to remind us, God is ever present. The Lords Prayer, is cherishing the sacrifice of His Son, removing the judgement of our sin, while God gives us the opportunity to follow His lead. The ultimate goal in prayer is to acknowledge God as our Creator and Surpreme Being, then live according to His will. Prayer is heard, in the power of His loving presence and will always bring an answer; yes, no, or wait. Having experienced all of these answers; sometimes questioning why? God's Holy Spirit gave me more detail …'Let His will be done!

Resting in God's promises of love, with true belief, no matter what happens in our life, we will soon be transformed in paradise forever, protected from all unhappy events. Believing in Jesus as our Savior, redeems us from the judgement and punishment of our misdeeds. Simply yielding to His presence in faith., our commitment to God in prayer, does not always go as we plan… but His response to our appeal always remains; yes, a no, or wait.

God reveals His deep love for us, as we put our faith in Him and trust in… "His Will." The outcome of any prayer, can be assured in resolution, as God leads to prepare a place for us in His kingdom. Meanwhile He is testing our faith, using our free will, to guide us to commune with Him and trust Him, which should sincerely come from our heart and soul.

Why Are We Here? Life as a human is much more complex than just living and dying. Long life is not guaranteed for any of us. Judging life as humans, we may live long enough to become wrinkled and old, or be taken earlier, according to God's will. The simplicity in life for me, rests upon the written Word of God, 'the Bible'. Consider life today, compared to the beginning of life on this planet., is there any similarity to then and now? The process of worldly change is remarkable. The environment, and traditions have certainly changed, dramatically. However, It seems the flesh of mankind remains the same. The Bible says the flesh profits nothing, it is our spirit living in us that controls our destiny, as we do evil or good. The truth of our flesh profits nothing, and cannot please God.! God's Word defines us as a spirit within us, created from the similarity of God's Spirit. It is my hope you will consider the reason for life, and the magnificent source of where your spirit comes from. Considering Creation, I am overwhelmed how much the power of Nature can lift my spirit. Pondering the balance of life on this planet seems to demonstrate many things in hope and happiness. It is easy to find joy in our existence. So the following is an example of God's work to study and realize the beauty and balance of our existence.

Human Life Cycle: We do not consider difficult challenges in life, until they happen. Some born with abnormal limitations, do not consider what could have been, but demonstrate the ability to live as a unique person. Humans control their abilities to function, as they are free to do so. But the 'insect' is given life to procreate for balance in nature.. Their existence is specific, with no other choice. Throughout the human life cycle, the body constantly changes, living through different periods of time, known as stages. The major stages of the human lifecycle are defined as follows: Fetus: The development of a zygote, into an embryo, progressing to a fetus for childbirth, produces the beginning of life as we know it. Neonate: After birthing, neonate denotes the first year of life. Infancy: The earliest part of childhood. It is the period from birth through age one. Toddler: Occurs between ages two and three. Childhood: Takes place from ages four to eight. Puberty: The period from ages nine to thirteen, is the beginning of adolescence. Older adolescence: The stage that takes place between ages fourteen and eighteen. Adulthood: The period from adolescence to the end of life, begins at age nineteen. Middle-age: The period of adulthood that stretches from age thirty-one to fifty. Old age: Extend from age fifty-one until the end of life.

Resources to Life During our lifetime: what resources are available to reach an acceptable result in difficult situations? We must look within ourselves to find the best approach to overcome strenuous times. Experiencing unwanted physical change, the emotion of fear may capture our attention. Some of us avoid the thought of life after death, and steer clear of any form of religion. Others cling to their faith in hope of moving on after this life is finished. So what is the answer to why we are here? The following lowing is something to consider.

Religions in the world: According to Google, total approximately 4,300. Among these totals, are the top 20 largest religions and their number of believers, some are without percentage, but appear in numbers:

1. Christianity (2.1 billion, 31.2%)
2. Islam (1.3 billion 24.1%)
3. Nonreligious (Secular/Agnostic/Atheist,) 1.1 billion 16%)
4. Hinduism (900 million, 15.1%)
5. Chinese traditional religion (394 million)
6. Buddhism (376 million, 6.9%)
7. Primal-indigenous (300 million)
8. African traditional (100 million)
9. Sikhism (23 million, 0.3 %)
10. Juche (19 million)
11. Spiritism (15 million)
12. Judaism (14 million)
13. Bahai (7 million)
14. Jainism (4.2 million)
15. Shinto (4 million)
16. Cao Dai (4 million)
17. Zoroastrianism (2.6 million)
18. Tenrikyo (a New Japanese religion, 2 million)
19. Neo-Paganism (1 million)
20. Unitarian-Universalism (800,000)

Note, The top three in religions are: 1) Christianity, 2) Islam, and 3) Nonreligious; totaling 4.5 billion people 71.3% of the Worlds population.

Verity of beliefs: Knowing Christians and the separation from the nonreligious sector, it is curious why Islam is so popular, as they also believe in a surpreme being, while all others do not.

Today: There are only about 14 million Jewish believers in the world. Which may indicate why there is always, a God kept remanent, keeping God's covenant with the Jews; as promised. What is the connections between abrahamic faiths and the Jews?

Abraham is traditionally considered to be the first Jew to have made a covenant with God. Because Judaism, Christianity, and Islam all recognize Abraham as their first prophet, they are also called the Abrahamic religions. While there was always a small community of Jews in historic Palestine; On May 14, 1948: David Bengurion, the head of the Jewish Agency, proclaimed the establishment of the 'State of Israel'. The United States President Harry S. Truman recognized the new nation on the same day.. The 70th Gregorian anniversary of the creation of the modern State of Israel, was relocated from its previous site in Tel Aviv, by the Donald Trump Administration, and is situated in the Arnon section of the United States Constitute. When my son-in-law Greg, a pastor, told me to keep a close eye on this little nation under the influence of God's power and strength, he said; God's plan is to guide them under the protection of His covenant with Abraham. This speaks volumes of their worth! Thank you Greg, for your deep compassion toward this little, but powerful country. Bless you for the many tours you have provided over the years. You have exposed many, to the true faith. Also, God Bless all pastors that teach the Word of God, verse by verse, chapter by chapter, book by book, keeping order, in the presentation of God's intent… to claim us after our death.

Islam and Christianity:

Islam was founded by an Arab merchant named Muhammed about AD 622. Muhammed claimed to have received a revelation from an angel of God, and, although he initially feared his revelation had come from Satan, Muhammed later claimed to be the last and greatest of all of God's prophets. Muhammed had **fifteen wives** (although he limited other men to four wives apiece) and sanctioned the beating of wives Muhammed was **well known for spreading his new religion by force.** He commanded, **"Fight and slay the Pagans wherever you find them,"** and he **specified the proper way to execute an unbeliever** was to cut his throat. Muhammed **led raids against caravans to plunder their goods, broke oaths, ordered the murder of those who mocked him, and wiped out the last Jewish tribe in Medina—he killed all the men and enslaved the women and children.** Interestingly, Muhammed acknowledged his own **need to seek God's forgiveness on occasion.** In stark contrast to the moral depravity of Muhammed, we now look at Jesus!

Christianity: Jesus Christ was above reproach in every way. Jesus never married, He defended and honored women, and His law was too, "love one another." Accordingly, Jesus never assassinated anyone, never beat a woman, never enslaved a child, never broke a promise, and never plundered a caravan. On the cross, when Jesus was mocked by those nearby, His response was, **"Father, forgive them."**

The Jewish Nation:

Being the Twelfth Nation in the world does not to go unnoticed. In addition to Christianity, the Jewish nation, now about 14 million people, were and are, befriended by God, who made a covenant with them, that would lead to Jesus Christ…the Messiah, the Son of God, become our personal Savior!

We must consider the power of God using a covenant with Abram (a Jew), calling the Messiah, Jesus Christ (a Jew), re-naming Abram to Abraham, (a Jew) applying His covenant to all nations. **This includes 'us'**, a mixed bag of non Jews called **Gentiles (non Jews)**. Giving us us an opportunity to believe and be part of God Kingdom! or face the consequences of Hell.

The Sign of the Covenant: Genesis 17: 1-10 NKJ When Abram was ninety-nine years old, the Lord appeared to Abram and said to him, "I am]Almighty God; walk before Me and be blameless. And I will make My covenant between Me and you, and will multiply you exceedingly." Then Abram fell on his face, and God talked with him, saying: "As for Me, behold, My covenant is with you, and you shall be a father of many nations. No longer shall your name be called Abram, but your name shall be Abraham; for I have made you a father of many nations. I will make you exceedingly fruitful; and I will make nations of you, and kings shall come from you. And I will establish My covenant between Me and you and your descendants after you in their generations, for an everlasting covenant, to be God to you and your descendants after you. Also I give to you and your descendants after you the land in which you are a stranger, all the land of Canaan, as an everlasting possession; and I will be their God." And God said to Abraham: "As for you, you shall keep My covenant, you and you're descendants after you throughout their generations. This is My covenant which you shall keep, between Me and you and your descendants after you.."

Considering the Truth: It is interesting that Christianity 2.1 billion, and Islam 1.3 billion inhabitants in the world, have faith that is controlled by a Superior invisible being, all others take a different path. Does Muhammad, appear to be gleaning from God's written word? Also;The Jewish people receiving this Covenant, has only 14 million people, as the 12th highest religion in the World. If you read God's word, you will find the source providing the absolute truth, through prophesy and history over time. It is fascinating that their position in all religions, include the number "12," which might be a sign from God as the 12 tribes of Israel. The actual life death and resurrection of Jesus Christ, was predicted in time, long before it actually happened. It is well documented in the Old Testament, as Jesus is confirmed, long before His time. With the guidance we have in God's word, especially regarding the Messiah, it is easy for me to believe in the life, death and resurrection of Jesus, when time changed from BC to AD; 2022 years ago. No other religion, makes it so easy to get access, to the powerful "after life.", as Jesus opened the door to paradise, giving us opportunity, to believe and trust in His existence, then follow His way to euphoria !

Jesus Christ, the Messiah: With His example of love and service, sacrificed himself, as God; becoming human flesh, without sin as both God and Man. He freed us from the punishment of our wrong doings (sin), that could not be resolved by any other way, than His loving sacrifice, as we believe in Him! I have not found any other way to the promise of everlasting life...except by the written word of God... and His saving grace; through the shed blood of His Son;...the innocent pure, loving Son of God.

Can You believe his? Understanding God's word, is like a marriage, establishing a new life, Submitting to the commandments of Gods will... to honor and serve, 'until death do us part... is our goal! However, the faithful who believe in Jesus, will not die, but have everlasting life. in the Kingdom, of Heaven… Jesus has set us Free! We are all forgiven, as we believe from our heart; Jesus is our Savior. His sacrifice removed the punishment of sin forever. During His time in the flesh, He remained pure and holy, committed to dying on the cross, to gather His believers, then return us to the Heavenly realm, without punishment of sin.

Love: The premise of love exists, because God exists in love,. with mercy, with grace, with truth. with power and compassion.. He is our triune God, Father, Son and Holy Spirit. God created us to have free choice, to follow His loving ways, or be banished from Him forever, in a place called Hell, all because they do not know Him

Created us, He incapsulates both good and evil, in this world. As we attempt to understand the difference, We are not able to battle for either, good or evil, because we are not God. Eventually Jesus gave us freedom… taking all of our sin upon Himself, to free us from punishment of the dark. He is the light, as we choose us to follow Him, until the celestial war is over; and the last believer is saved. Then anew earth without evil can be created.

Your Choice: Believe or not believe, is a very simple choice. If we choose to believe Jesus is our Savior, as we depend on following His will, we are free from the punishment of our sin, and given the opportunity to understand God's true love…who provides life without evil, suffering or Pain.! As we believe in Jesus to serve others in love, our accomplishments will be rewarded in heaven during the final judgement.

When we die: Considering transformation after the death of our flesh, our life is transformed into our Spirit. Jesus is our guiding light. He is the only means to pass through the narrow gate, to enter Heaven forever, in peace and joy. However, those of us who claim to be Christians, may not be as true in their belief as they might think. To be a Christian, there are two commandments that lead us in our faith; "Love God with all your heart, and to love others as God loves you." This is considered the two greatest commandments, among all that exist. This short version of truth is centered on belief the Bible, is written by God Himself. We must commit our full attention to following Jesus Christ as our Savior. He is the only way to heaven. As a pure man without sin, as He consumed our punishment. So we can now follow His will to be saved, or disregard His presence and be separated from Him forever. Claiming Christianity' is futile if we do not engage in the presence of our Lord. A personal and meaningful relationship with Jesus is essential to being saved through process of God's will, by believing in your heart…otherwise: He will not know you. There are many who claim to be Christians, falling short in being a true believer. Also, attending Church or just claiming the name of Jesus, falls short in understanding…God wants a relationship with us, that confirms from the heart, we truly believe.

Renewal: Over the years, my life has changed dramatically. As I commune with God throughout each day; praying without ceasing is God's way of telling me to acknowledge His presence, that never goes away. God comes to my mind throughout each day, in connection to life its-self. His presence, is always on the move in our life. As we commune with Him frequently, our thoughts encounter questionable needs reacting to changing events. Faith and communication are focused on God, who makes an ideal way to concur His existence, using our prayers to guide self or others to; 'Pray without ceasing)!

Among the many changes we face, the most difficult is adjusting to alternatives in physical and emotional well being. Common illnesses are tolerable, because we are confident they will pass in a short period of time. However, there are other situations that may challenge your life forever. Overcoming or adjusting to these events is difficult. Success will depend on how you approach a different way of "compromised needs.". Unwanted change increases our anxiety and fear. Why? Because we did not plan for it! Our demeanor is to pursue happiness. Unexpected change, is not considered until it happens. Without previous planning or direction, the individual participants find themselves in a dilemma of how to rekindle stability.

It is Up to Us: Our ability to adapt to changing events, rests on us as individuals. Life is personal., and adjustments must be made to our satisfaction. As we seek a new goal to regain comfort and stability. there are many who give up their fight for a suitable compromise in favor of; substance abuse, reclusion, or suicide; avoiding positive things, they are not capable of controlling. It is up to us to choose our future, no matter what happens next. Compromising situations are common in everyday life. Most are easily resolved choosing between several options. However with abrupt physical change, options are limited to adjustment and time, producing a prolonged period of anxiety, until motivation and acceptance is established.

Encouragement from Jesus: 2 Corinthians 1:3-5 NKJ : "Blessed be the God and Father of our Lord Jesus Christ; the Father of mercies and God of all comfort; who comforts us in all our tribulation, that we may be able to comfort those who are in any trouble, with the same comfort which we ourselves are comforted by God. For as the sufferings of Christ abound in us, so our consolation also abounds, through Christ".

Faith prevails in all changes: Matthew 6:25 NKJ: "Look at the birds in the air; they do not sow or reap or store away in barns, and yet your heavenly Father feeds them. Are you not much more valuable than they?" We do not look back to what was… but look forward to what is! Adjust to daily events, pressing forward to what you can do, rather than dwell on what you cannot do. Accept your limits, and gain confidence in your abilities; understand; life is short and some of those experiencing unwanted or prolonged change, need to find peace in their situation to be successful or fail in despair.

Seek God: Matthew 6:26-33 NKJ " Therefore do not worry, saying, 'What shall we eat?' or 'What shall we drink?' or 'What shall we wear?' For after all these things the Gentiles seek. For your heavenly Father knows that you need all these things. But seek first the kingdom of God and His righteousness, and all these things shall be added to you" If God cares for the non human life in His Creation; will He not also look after us.? Stay close to his lead, and remember, by faith you will prevail.

Review: Top Three Religions: According to the top three religions, Christianity, Islam, and Non-religious, occupy a little more than half of the worlds population. This gives opportunity to choose your faith, in consideration to ponder, what might be the truth to believe in or not. It is choice to believe any of them, or not.

Christianity: " The faith that Believes in one God: The Father Almighty, Maker of heaven, and earth, and the sea, and all things that are in them; along with Christ Jesus, the Son of God, who became incarnate for our salvation; and the Holy Spirit who displays direction in the way we should go, that captures the good in what God wants from us, given to us by Jesus to follow His lead. The definition of Christianity from the Bible: (A) The religion derived from Jesus Christ, based on the Bible as sacred scripture, and professed by Eastern, Roman Catholic, and Protestant bodies. (B) conformity to the Christian religion (C) The practice of Christianity. When did Christianity begin? Christianity originated with the ministry of Jesus in the Roman province of Judea. According to the Gospels, Jesus was a Jewish teacher and healer who proclaimed the imminent kingdom of God; and was crucified, claiming a new change in Belief. His life is recorded from His birth as man in the Old Testament. Also, changing world history time,. to BC and AD, Acknowledging His Devine presence as the Son of God. Also as a reminder: The Old Testament claims the Messiah, as Jesus, and Other recordings of actual events, long before they Happened. This prophecy solidifies the truth of God, and His Word, as the only God of mankind!.

Islam: What is the real meaning of Islam? Islam is an Arabic word meaning "submission" and in a religious context means "submission to the will of God". "Islam" is derived from the Arabic Word "Sal'm", which literally means 'peace'. The religion of which demonstrates peace and tolerance. The religion of the Muslims as monotheistic faith regarded and revealed through Muhammad, as the Prophet of Allah. When Muhammad was born in 570 AD**,** Christianity had spread widely but in their Holy Scriptures, but they found no mention of Muhammad., However Allah is described as God. "Who is Allah? What is the origin of belief in Allah?" Allah is an Arabic word that means "God" or, more accurately, "the God." In Western culture, it is commonly believed that the word Allah is used exclusively by Muslims to describe their god, but this is not actually true. The word Allah is used by Arabic speakers of all Abrahamic faiths (including Christianity and Judaism) as meaning "God." However, according to Islam, Allah is God's proper name, while Christians and Jews know Him as YHWH or Yahweh. When Arabic speaking Christians use the word Allah, it is usually used in combination with the word al-Ab. Allah al-Ab means "God the Father," and this usage is one way Arab Christians distinguish themselves separate from Muslims. What is the real meaning of Islam? Islam is an Arabic word meaning "submission" and in a religious context means "submission to the will of God". "Islam" is derived from the Arabis Word, " Sal'm", which literally means peace". The religion of which demonstrate peace and tolerance.

Non-religious atheist:

There is a key distinction; an atheist doesn't believe God or a divine being.

Agnostic: reveals a kind of religious in attitude to the universe: skeptic, doubter, challenger, scoffer, cynic; unbeliever, disbeliever, nonbeliever; rationalist; rare nullifidian.

Earth Religion: The most inspirational gifts from God is the fascinating power of nature. It is essential to life, without it, we cannot thrive. What if the Creator of nature revealed His glorified presence to commune with us? Nature is one of the many magnificent aspects of God's creation. The natural state of Nature has intrigued mankind for centuries. To this date there have been many discoveries, helping us understand the power and stability of nature, as connected to the balance of all life. There is an array of groups and beliefs that fall under earth religion. Paganism, which is a polytheistic, nature based religion; animism, which is the worldview that all living entities (plants, animals, and humans) possess a spirit; 'Wicca', which hold the concept of an earth mother goddess, as well as practice Earth religion, a term used mostly in the context of neopaganism. Earth-centered religion or Nature worship, a system of religion based on the veneration of phenomena. It covers any religion that Worships the earth, Nature, or fertility deity , such as the various forms of goddess worship or matriarchal religion . Some find a connection between earth-worship and the Gaia hypothesis, (a synergistic and self-regulating complex system , that helps to maintain and perpetuate the conditions for life on the planet). Earth religions are also formulated to allow one to utilize the knowledge of preserving the earth Earth- religion.

The Power of Nature: What keeps our environment balanced? Where does the form of nature come from… if not from a Devine Creator? Nature is designed for all of mankind to ponder its magnificent beauty, questioning how it came to be. The intricate arrangement of non-human life, gives us everything we need to control our future… without it, we would fail to exist. The complex balance for all things in Creation, arouses curiosity, and appears to be balanced by something, but what? I believe the God of the Bible, is the true source of our existence. Why? Because the written word in the Bible, is proven by its prophecy, predicting events and changes in our future, before they actually happened. Also the physical appearance of Jesus Christ himself who is both God and man. Appearing after His crucification ascending into heaven viewed by many witnesses. God's character is valued as our supreme being, presented as love, which proves itself, far and away from the written history of life on this planet. The combination of world history and the written word of God, proves or Spiritual Father exists. Nature is given to us by God's good pleasure. The boundaries we live in, do not reveal where God come from. The probability of His existence is found only in the book He wrote; the Bible. Claiming to be the great, "I Am". I have no desire to focus on where God came from. My belief is… He exists. God provides us with an inspirational glimpse of how the balance of nature effects our ability to flourish.

What would it be like: Without His presence? Nature is essential to life on this planet, reminding us of a complexity we cannot completely understand or control. What if God appeared to us in His Glorified Spirit? Would we be thrilled He exists? Encouraged to live in His kingdom forever? Without conflict or change? To dwell with Him as His children? Being like Him in Spirit? Having everlasting love to guide us throughout eternity? Are you ready to meet Him?

Act of God: The natural state if nature has intrigued mankind for centuries. Some findings are proven truthful, but many claims rest more on theory rather than fact. Mishaps in nature, regarding natural disasters, is a threat to all of mankind. Many household insurance companies in the United States, have an 'act of God claim' that omits payment, with disasters out of their control, or encourages additional fee's in recognized in areas of repeated natural disasters. What we fail to see is the natural realm of nature, that controls all life on this planet. Reading and understanding, the God of the Bible, I find no other thing to believe in because of its viable truth… God is in charge of it all. Who is God and what is His will? The will of God, divine will, or God's plan, is the concept of God having a plan for humanity. Ascribing a volition or a plan to a god generally is implied personal. A God regarded as a person with mind, emotions, and will. (Will of God Wikipedia.) What Wikipedia leaves out, is the plan for God to gather all of humanity into His Kingdom, forever!. However, not everyone will get that opportunity, simply because they do not believe in Him, or His word, the Bible. It is my intent to offer the reality of a Devine Creator, as the answer to find peace, stability and truth, all presented by the power of God's Word, and also His presence. Created by God's love, we cannot please our Creator without having truth, love, trust, and the expectation that He exists. The truth of God's Son, Jesus (living as man-God), dying on the cross to remove the judgement of our sin, also secures His promise of everlasting life, as we believe and follow His message. God gives us the promise of life after death. As we believe the resurrection of Jesus; He guides us to be with Him forever. We must truthfully confide in Him…spirit to spirit, and recognize His tremendous love for us is personal, as He prepares us for everlasting life in Heaven. The simplicity of acknowledging Jesus is your Savior, truly convinced, He is our gateway to heaven, secures an extraordinary effect for future; after death!

The God of the Bible: According to His written word, God is not only a person, but a being. What does that mean? He claims to be our God of Spirit, the Supreme being over everything in His Creation; claiming Himself As, "The Great I AM " there is no other! God exists in love, against evil, and those who refuse to believe in Him, will be removed from His presence forever. A person lives and dies, but the God of the Bible, claims to be an eternal spirit. By His word, humans die to release their Spirit, then return to God's Kingdom for judgement or reward. God sent His Son to remove the judgement of our sin, (sin: anything that stands between us and God's will). Believing in the Sacrifice of Jesus, truthfully from our heart, we are saved by His head blood; justified to enter heaven, as we place our faith in Him. Jesus has given us a passage as we claim His deity as our Savior. Our Spirit was born in the garden prepared by God. Adam was the first and Eve followed as a companion to spiritual life. The couple dwelt in the garden, having free choice to everything, accept the tree in center of the Garden, called the tree of knowledge of good and evil. By avoiding this tree, of good and evil, Adam and Eve did well in the spirit. However God gave them a free choice in the gift of life, to ponder His love, but also offered a choice to follow His will, or be captured in the flesh to die in darkness. God's will is to avoid evil by staying in the light or be placed in darkness forever. Satan is the king of darkness, and remains 'the reason for our fall'. Not following God's will, having a free choice, believing or not, God removed Adam and Eve as free spirits in heaven, to toil and thrive in the flesh, then eventually die and be judged in Spirit, toward everlasting life or the everlasting darkness of hell. God in His mercy remains in the love of His creation, wanting us to be in His kingdom, as we believe and follow. Choosing God's way or the Devils way… one or the other… is your choice, without partiality. Surrounded by the presence of evil, there is a spiritual battle, consuming many who refuse to believe in God. We all die in the flesh. When the flesh is gone, our lives as spirits does not fade away, but according to the Bible, is changed in the twinkling of an eye and transformed into spirit to be judged by God. If the Bible is true, some of us will live as immortal spirits, through the saving grace of Jesus, gaining love and peace; while others will be condemned forever, not believing in our Devine Creator, to love in darkness.

The Command to Love: 1 John 3:1-3 NKJ "Behold what manner of love the Father has bestowed on us, that we should be called children of God! Therefore the world does not know us, because it did not know Him. Beloved, now we are children of God; and it has not yet been revealed what we shall be, but we know that when He is revealed, we shall be like Him, for we shall see Him as He is, and everyone who has this hope in Him, purifies himself, just as He is pure."

Psalms 46 NKJ " God is our refuge and strength, A very present help in trouble. Therefore we will not fear. Even though the earth be removed, and though the mountains be carried into the midst of the sea; Though its waters roar and be troubled, Though the mountains shake with its swelling; there is a river whose streams shall make glad the City of God. The Holy place of the tabernacle of the Most High. God is in the midst of her, she shall not be moved; God shall help her, just at the break of dawn. The nations raged, the kingdoms were moved; He uttered His voice, the earth melted. The Lord of hosts is with us; the God of Jacob is our refuge. Come, behold the works of the Lord, who has made desolations in the earth. He makes wars cease to the end of the earth; He breaks the bow and cuts the spear in two; He burns the chariot in the fire. Be still, and know that I am God; I will be exalted among the nations, I will be exalted in the earth! The Lord of hosts is with us; the God of Jacob is our refuge."

Those not believing in the saving grace of Jesus, will stand in judgement. We cannot justify ourselves to live an eternal life, without claiming Jesus as ourSavior." God's word, is written by many authors, with historical ties to common history of the world, since the beginning of time. A diverse group of writers, coming out of three continents, describe many scenarios, to help us understand the reason for God's presence. The reason for His Creation, is His desire is to be loved, as He lives and loves us, without pain and sorrow, to enjoy the thrill of His presence. Jesus Christ, our Savior, received the judgement of our sin, omitting the punishment of sin we cannot avoid. Jesus is always present in our lives. Believing in Him, we are covered by His Holiness, free from the punishment of our sin forever, to be with God and enjoy the treasure of everlasting life, without evil. As both God and man, Jesus presents Himself with authority, proclaiming His Deity as an innocent man, and His Deity as God Himself. He gives us an opportunity to hear His Word to be saved. Refusing Him by our free will, the consequences of darkness, brings us to remain forever in Hell.

Consider a world of love and peace. Jesus gives us free will when dealing with choice. Denying Him of His powerful existence, we will be separated from Him forever. Jesus suffered and died for us, as a perfect God- man, without sin, wanting us to rejoin Him in God's Kingdom. The experience of true love, and freedom, are ours to choose, or reject.

Romans 7:18-25 NKJ " For I know that in me (that is, in my flesh) nothing good dwells; for to will is present with me, but how to perform what is good, I do not find. For the good that I will to do, I do not do; but the evil I will not to do, that I practice. Now if I do what I will not to do, it is no longer I who do it, but sin that dwells in me. I find then a law, that evil is present with me, the one who wills to do good. For I delight in the law of God according to the inward man. But I see another law in my members, warring against the law of my mind, and bringing me into captivity to the law of sin which, is in my members. O wretched man that I am! Who will deliver me from this body of death? I thank God through Jesus Christ our Lord!"

Reading Scripture: I believe and feel, all of this is true. Our personal feelings belong in all of us, to guide us through various events in life. From the Bible, God demonstrates His feeling toward mankind. He wants us to acknowledge Him and feel His Spirit dwelling within us. Those who believe in Him, will gain, peace on earth, and also the promise of everlasting life in the Heavenly realm., away from evil, for eternity.

Feeling: Studying the Bible in a mens group, after sharing my feelings and thoughts, one of the men claimed; faith is not a feeling! It was like a spear cutting through my heart, as I questioned… is not love a feeling? If God is love, is that not a feeling? How does love apply to faith? The Holy Spirit has counseled me to feel the power of God's love and intent, the power of his word, that instructs us to follow his way as written in his book. My thought is faith, is not an **opinion**, but a following to understand God's presence and His word. **Dictionary:** Faith, as a noun, is complete trust or confidence in someone or something. A strong belief in God or in the doctrines of a religion, based on spiritual apprehension, rather than proof. It is a system of religious belief .. As Christian's, can we 'feel' the presence of God in our lives? The word 'feel' as a verb, has many connotations: perceive, sense, detect, discern, make out, notice, observe, identify; be sensible of, have a sensation of, be aware of… so consider how to share your feelings, following the Word of God. Feeling by opinion can be the most devastating occurrence known to mankind, unless it is a truthful fact. The only truthful fact I know is God's word. My opinion, can be a choice, or a feeling, a fact, or a judgement of logic, or truth…so we must be careful to concur what is wright, or wrong as we give our opinion, feeling the truth of God's will to prevail.

Why do we study the Bible? To gain more faith in it's truth about our Creator? Do we truly believe in His existence? Are we in awe of Him? Is their truth in the spirits of men He Created? Reading His book, do we grow closer in understanding our Supreme Being? Is that a feeling? To follow Him in love, or succumb to follow hate and self indulgence, is that feeling? Flourishing from God's Word, He is invisible, so how can we feel His presence and draw near to Him?

Walk In the Spirit: What is a person's spirit? A person's spirit is the nonphysical part of us that is believed to remain alive after their death. Spirit is the courage and determination that helps people to survive in difficult times, to keep their way of life and their beliefs. (Collins English Dictionary)

1 Corinthians 2:9-12 NKJ " But as it is written: the Eye has not seen, nor ear heard, Nor have entered into the heart of man; the things which God has prepared for those who love Him. God has revealed them to us through His Spirit. For the Spirit searches all things, yes, the deep things in God. For what man knows the things of a man, except the spirit of the man which is in him? Even so, no one knows the things of God except the Spirit of God. Believing, we have received, not the spirit of the world; but the Spirit who is from God, that we might know the things that have been freely given to us by God. "

Romans 8:15-16 NKJ " For you did not receive the spirit of bondage again to fear, but you received the Spirit of adoption by whom we cry out, " Abba, Father." The Spirit Himself bears witness with our spirit that we are children of God."

1 John 3:1-3 NKJ "See what great love the Father has lavished on us, that we should be called children of God! And that is what we are! The reason the world does not know us is that it did not know 'Him'. ear friends, now we are children of God, and what we will be has not yet been made known. But we know that when Christ appears, we shall be like him, for we shall see him as he is. All who have this hope in him purify themselves, just as he is pure."

Ephesians 2:13-19 NKJ " But now in Christ Jesus you who once were far off have been brought near by the blood of Christ. Now, therefore, you are no longer strangers and foreigners, but fellow citizens with the saints and members of the household of God."

Romans 1: 10-12 NKJ " But if Christ is in you, then even though your body is subject to death because of sin, the Spirit gives life because of righteousness. And if the Spirit of him who raised Jesus from the dead is living in you, He who raised Christ from the dead will also give life to your mortal bodies because of His Spirit who lives in you. Therefore, brothers and sisters, we have an obligation—but it is not to the flesh, to live according to it. For if you live according to the flesh, you will die; but if by the Spirit you put to death the misdeeds of the body, you will live."

As I ponder scripture in the Bible; 'IF' the absolute truth does not come from God, why did He allow us to have free choice in managing our lives? Believing in Him or not, is the ultimate hope, in understanding the 'why' we are here!

Humans Numbered Like a Grain of Sand: Living in old age, my anticipation of Jesus calling me home, is getting surprisingly closer. All of us, living the life God has given us, can die at any moment. From the youngest embryo to the oldest aging person, we cannot escape death.

It is sometimes difficult for us to accept the varying changes in life, if we compare ourselves to the world.

Isaiah 48:17-19 NKJ "Thus says the Lord, our Redeemer, The Holy One of Israel, I am the Lord your God, who teaches you to profit, who leads you by the way you should go. Oh, that you had heeded My commandments! Then your peace would have been like a river, and you're righteousness like the waves of the sea. Your descendants also would have been like the sand, and the offspring of your body like the grains of sand; His name would not have been cut off, Nor destroyed from before Me." As we are compared to a grains of sand in number, from God's word. imagine how big God is, as he holds our Universe in the palm of His hand? If we contrast earth, with the smallest star in the universe, it is like putting a golfball (representing earth), next to the Empire State building, in New York City, (representing the smallist star). Comparing mankind, being like grains of sand, is appropriate in size, as we consider the mass of Earth compared to Heaven. To God, we are more than just minuscule in mass, we are loved as spirits, created in His image, reminding us, when we separate from the flesh, to our spirit, we will commune with God's Spirit, as we live forever tin His Kingdom.

Reflection: Take a moment to think about the world around you. What do you see? What amazes you when it comes to the intricate balance of all life on this planet? Including the variety of plants, trees and the variation of area in which they grow. The variety of intricate design, includes the movement of living creatures, from the smallest of biological discoveries, to the largest of animals, in addition to an incredible diversification of vegetation by land or sea. Recently my wife was at the grocery store and discovered some daffodil bulbs arranged in a vase, using water only, to grow and be planted in the spring. After one week in our home, in the middle of winter, I took the following picture:

Looking at this photo, being dazzled by the artistic work of this plant, seeing its roots below, remarkable veins in the bulbs, the towers of green leaves, and a touch of colorful yellow flowers… "Joy to the world" seems to be appropriate. Also my wife's collection of winter characters, bring this display to awe, in the beauty of life, free from turmoil and frustration. The question is: How did all of Creation come to be?

"The Grape from God:" I was nothing, then I am. A seedling to be planted, nurtured to grow, watered and fed waiting to be, a beautiful fruit, pleasing to see. Learning to know you, as I remain, feeling the blessing of the sun and the rain, Life can be wonderful, or sad at times, being young, or growing old. Now I am wrinkled meeting your goal, pleasing the maker of my soul, Knowing the power of Your creation, I once was a grape, but now, I am a raisin.! (Ed Conine 2014)

Value: This little poem gives me a glimpse of life. We are planted in our mothers womb and allowed to grow, becoming human in a world of desirable life. But, as our youth fades, touched by the pearls of life, we will eventually consider what is life all about? We live and we die, but we are blessed by a loving Creator. Believing in God; we will be changed unlike the grape', to be something else. According to the Bible our Spirit living in us will be revealed at death… as who we truly are! When we die, there is a metaphor revealing the action of this event found in nature. The life of a moth or butterfly is exciting to discover. Unlike the grape, God gives us an example of transforming from one life to another. A crawling insect (caterpillar), turning into a beautiful flying creature (moth or butterfly), are a strong example of what will happen when we reach the end of this cocoon we live in.

The Moth and the Butterfly: The butterfly and moth uniquely change from one form to another. They are also assigned to benefit other living things in the balance of nature. If we compare mankind to all creatures in the world, there is no comparison who dominates life as we know it. As Humans our talents, abilities, and power, not only have jurisdiction over the creatures on earth, but additionally we have been given the ability to adjust, to consider options, as we battle personal obstacles through changing events.

What is a caterpillar? A caterpillar is the larval form of a butterfly or a moth. When butterflies and moths lay eggs, the eggs hatch as caterpillars. This caterpillar is a baby butterfly or a baby moth. We know that butterflies and moths are insects. Does this mean that the caterpillars are separate insects from butterflies or moths? If not, they can still be noticed as two different creatures coming from one source… one crawls and one flies. How much does a caterpillar need to eat

Imagine a seven-pound newborn child consuming 1400 pounds of formula in a two-week period. Commercial butterfly breeders tell me that each Monarch caterpillar can easily defoliate an entire one-gallon milkweed plant–consuming 175-200 leaves per caterpillar–before enclosing to the chrysalis stage. **(Google)**

Cocoon, vs. Chrysalis: :It's common to call the shell where a butterfly completes its metamorphosis as a cocoon, but that's technically incorrect. While some insects, like moths, spin a cocoon, a butterfly uses a chrysalis, which is essentially hardened skin. (Google) What do butterflies and moths eat? With few exceptions, adult butterflies and moths eat only various liquids to maintain their water balance and energy stores. Most adults sip flower nectar, but others imbibe fluids from sap, flowers on trees, rotting fruits, bird droppings, or animal dung.(www.kidsbutterfly.org/faq/behavior/

What is the time frame before birth? Different species of butterflies stay in the chrysalis, or pupal stage, in different periods of time. This can range from about seven days to more than a year, but for a large number of species it is less than thirty days. The well-known monarch butterfly, for example, spends between nine and fourteen days in a chrysalis, while the painted lady butterfly spends only seven to days in the chrysalis. Butterflies have four distinct stages in their life cycle. They start as an egg, hatch into a caterpillar, turn into pupae during metamorphosis, and finally emerge as a butterfly. Consider the larva as an egg, how do you explain why it eventually grows legs and moves? What is explanation in the change from a ground creature to one of flight? What are the benefits in nature, from the life of a caterpillar, butterfly or moth? What is the value of a moth, other than to play around porch light and eat your clothes?

Research: In a TV documentary called Nature, they claimed there are over twenty thousand different species of butterflies and moths. This illustrates the wonder of God's creation, as we compare them to the diverse population of the world. The scientific explanation for butterfly or moth is that they are part of the food chain as a major diet for bats, as well as many other creatures. "They also benefit plants by pollinating flowers or crops, while feeding on their nectar, which helps in seed production. They benefit wild plants, but also much of our food crops depend on moths and butterflies, with other insects, to ensure a good harvest. "(Google)

Note: After reviewing this information, it is interesting to see how the flow of science is attempting to clarify the process of life around us, as in the case of the moth and butterfly. Consider the larva as an egg, how do you explain why it eventually grows legs and moves? What is the explanation in the change from a ground creature to one of flight? What are the benefits in nature, coming from the life of a caterpillar or butterfly or moth? How does this example of an insect, compare to the process of our human life?

Inevitable Change: As we consider the process of life by age, it is interesting to ponder memories, as time go's bye. We do not consider difficult challenges in life, until they happen. Some born with abnormal limitations, do not consider what could have been, but demonstrate the ability to live as a unique person. Pain and suffering is not a happy life. As you read on, it is my intention to expose the difficulty in altered physical conditions, and questionable emotional in states of mind; toward a new way of living.

Recovery: When experiencing physical or emotional loss, instability will require much of our instinct to find acceptance, and peace. Strength is needed toward accepting change, which can sometimes be devastating. Using pros and cons, is necessary to find a new path toward contentment. Questioning situations, striving to find the ability to tolerate change, is a personal battle. First by accepting your particular circumstances, then trying to find resolution, as you consider goals and options committing to stability. What are the resources available to gain an acceptable compromise? We must look within ourselves, for the best approach to overcome tragic circumstances. Unwanted physical change brings the emotion of fear, capturing our attention, in what to do next? Adjustments are essential for success. After grieving period of time, accepting the situation, the struggle of rehabilitation begins. Personal values and beliefs are fundamental in the journey of recovery. Tolerance to the unknown or the unseen, is necessary, as one gathers adjustment to find an outcome that is suitable, tolerable, and excepted as a new way to approach to life. Caring for those who have unexpected trauma, especially on the edge of death, my faith allows me to pray for the best possible recovery from medical intervention. Identifying and meeting the concerns of the patient, suggests family support is a valuable asset to include in the process of recovery. One of my biggest concerns in caring for my patients, is to keep the family involved in the flow leading to adjustment and strength. In the business of medical intervention, caretakers may seem to forget the value of family, because they are often caught up in stabilizing their selected group of patients, which keeps them on the move. Focusing on patients who need immediate attention, or prolonged treatments, is decided by priority. For me, welcoming family at the bedside to observe treatment and educate them on progress, it is encouraging for both patient and family. As nurses we work with priority by need. Those who are stable with lower priority will benefit from visiting family and friends, as the nurse cares for a higher priority patient. Family is an important resource to help maintain balance in the patients recovery. If observed to be helpful, and not having a negative responses to the patient and staff, they should be welcomed.

All nurses are valuable, with deep concern for their patients, but at the end of their day, there is still more to do, and some things in their charge, are passed on to the incoming caretaker. There have been many times, when leaving the Hospital, I felt like a failure, because of not having the time to do all things for my patients. But the system is good, because the next caretaker will follow up on what was not accomplished.

The most important part of my career was experiencing grief and despair, found patients and family. My compassion grew stronger as time moved on. Some patients were living in a war zone, needing continued reassurance, especially from family, to tolerate their circumstances. During these times I would often allow family a longer visit, giving support to their loved one. The time limit for visiting was short, so I was criticized by my peers, having visitors stay longer. However this occurred only if they would include the patient, as the central figure of the visit. Otherwise they were excused. Many times during the season of my employment, I prayed silently to God for success in healing, not only for physical needs, but also for their spiritual needs as well.

Religion: The number one religion in this world is Christianity. filled with love and compassion. The Christen Bible and its Historical presentation, includes life after death. Reading its content, I believe God is, who He says He is! All humans are sinful and unable to commune with God who is sinless. Jesus, communing with God, volunteered to save the sinful, for the ability to return to Gods kingdom. He 0set us free free from our misdeeds, by consuming all sin, past present and future, sacrificing Himself for the punishment, of our sin, we can not battle on our own. Being both eternal and human , Jesus set us free, reconciling all sin to Himself… as an innocent sacrificial lamb.. He gives opportunity for those who believe, to be free from deserved punishment.

What does Jesus do for us? Jesus opens the gateway to Heaven. Believing in Him, we will be transformed after death to live a new life as we release our flesh to reveal our Spirit. I believe my spirit, is me!

Uniquely made, like no other. I will be given a new name, identifying my relationship with Jesus, that no one else can claim! Jesus is the only means for us to pass through the narrow gate into eternity; convinced by His word, to all who commit to his calling. Unfortunately, those of us who claim to be Christians, may not be as true in our belief, as we might think. To be a Christian, there are two commandments that lead us in our faith. 'To Love God with all your heart, and to love your neighbors as as your self.' These two greatest commandments communicate the standards we should follow. As we sin, knowing we are saved by the blood shed of Jesus (avoiding judgement), there is another step to follow called repentance. What is repentance? Reaching out to God in prayer, in remorse, acknowledging an error in conduct of faith, as we turn to God for forgiveness; identifying our misdeeds. Jesus who set free from our sin., acknowledges our need to reconcile our misdeeds, and followup making condolences to God. Whether right or wrong, having sincere regret, should guide us in in the challenge of love.

The Bible is written by God Himself: The power of Gods written word cannot be disclaimed. The Bible also mixes well with world history. Having forty authors, from three continents, writing God's word, they follow history and prophesy in combined proof of its content. The writings are true, and cannot be disproved!

2 Timothy 1:7 NKJ " For God has not given us a spirit of fear, but of power and of love and of a sound mind." **John 14:17, 26 NKJ** " The Spirit of truth, whom the world cannot receive, because it neither sees Him nor knows Him; but you know Him, for He dwells with you and will be in you. But the Helper, the Holy Spirit, whom the Father will send in My name, He will teach you all things, and bring to your remembrance all things that I said to you. Thanks be to God, who always leads us to triumph in Christ, for we are to God, the fragrance of Christ, among those who are being saved and among those who are perishing."

Sonship Through the Spirit: Romans 8:9-11 NKJ " But you are not in the flesh, but in the Spirit, if indeed the Spirit of God dwells in you. Now if anyone does not have the Spirit of Christ, he is not His." We must commit our full attention to following Jesus Christ as our Savior, He is the way to heaven. We are lead by the Holy Spirit to stay on track in following God's Will of love. **Romans 8: 12-17 NKJ** "Therefore, brethren, we are debtors—not to the flesh, to live according to the flesh; for if you live according to the flesh you will die; but if by the Spirit you put to death the deeds of the body… you will live. For as many as are led by the Spirit of God, these are sons of God. For you did not receive the spirit of bondage again to fear, but you received the Spirit of adoption by whom we cry out, "Abba, Father." The Spirit Himself bears witness with our spirit that we are children of God, and if children, then heirs of God; and joint heirs with Christ, if indeed we suffer with Him, that we may also be glorified together".

Claiming Christianity: Life is futile if we do not engage; knowing that the presence and power of God is everlasting. As we establish a meaningful relationship with Him, believing from our heart and soul, the pathway He provides is by His Will; otherwise, He will not know us.

Food for thought: There are Two and one half billion people, claiming to be Christians. But it might render a different number far less than printed; mostly because some lack complete faith in the growing process of understanding God's Word and His Will; to serve mankind with love. By works of faith, trusting in His Word; is followed by the promise of being with Him, forever in eternity.

Environment: The most inspirational gifts from God, come from the fascinating power of nature, essential to life; without it we cannot thrive. What if the Creator of nature revealed His glorified presence? Nature is only one of the many magnificent aspects in God's creation. The natural state of Nature has intrigued mankind for centuries, and to this date there have been many discoveries, helping us understand the power and stability connected to the balance of all life.

Questioning Life? What keeps our environment balanced? Where does the form of nature come from, if not from a Devine Creator? Nature is designed for all of mankind to ponder its magnificent beauty. Questioning how it came to be, is fascinating. The intricate arrangement of non-human life, gives us everything we need to control our future…without it, we would fail to exist. The complex balance for all things in creation, arouses curiosity and appears to be balanced by something; but what? I believe the God of the Bible, is the true source of our existence. Why? Because the written word in the Bible, is proven to be true by its prophecy, predicting events and changes in our future before they actually happened. The Bible is the most incredible event of truth in God's character, valued as our Supreme Being Nature is given to us by God's love and pleasure. The boundaries we live in, do not reveal where God come from; but the probability of His existence is found only in the book He wrote…the Bible. Claiming to be the great, "I Am"; I have no desire to focus on where God came from. My belief is… He exists! God provides us with an inspirational glimpse of how the balance of nature effects our ability to flourish. What would it be like, without His presence? Nature is essential to life on this planet; reminding us we cannot completely understand or control, this complex system, that devastates our environment without warning or reason. What if God appeared to us in His Glorified Spirit? Would we be thrilled He exists? Are we ready to live in His kingdom forever without conflict or change? Just by believing in Jesus? To dwell with Him as His children? Being like Him in Spirit, having everlasting love to guide us throughout eternity? The natural state of nature has intrigued mankind throughout centuries. . Some things have been proven truthful, however some are in 'theory' rather than fact. Theory keeps our guesswork questionable. Mishaps in nature are known natural disasters, threatening mankind in his natural environment. Many household insurance companies in the United States have an 'act of God' clause in their policies, omitting or reducing compensated payment, in disasters out of their control.

The Uniqueness of God: In the first book of the Bible, God demonstrates His power by taking a faithful family and many animals, on a cruse, in a boat, guided and built by His servant Noah. Giving mankind a free will; God knew Satan was overpowering humans by his influence of evil. After the fall of Adam and Eve; the power of Satan continued to produce evil in the world. Gods reaction to this, was not to destroy mankind altogether, but keep a remnant for His good pleasure. After finding a new place for His chosen ones, God established a reason to celebrate His works in the message of the rainbow. Excerpts from this event is as follows: **Genesis 5:32 NKJ** And Noah was five hundred years old, and Noah begot Shem, Ham, and Japheth. **Genesis 6:8 NKJ** But Noah found grace in the eyes of the Lord. **Genesis 6:9 NKJ** This is the genealogy; Noah was a just man, perfect in his generation. Noah walked with God.

Genesis 6:13-16 NKJ: "And God said to Noah, the end of all flesh has come before Me, for the earth is filled with violence through them; and behold, I will destroy them with the earth. Make yourself an ark of gopherwood; make rooms in the ark, and cover it inside and outside with pitch. And this is how you shall make it: The length of the ark shall be three hundred cubits, its width fifty cubits, and its height thirty cubits. You shall make a window for the ark, and you shall finish it to a cubit from above; and set the door of the ark in its side. You shall make it with lower, second, and third decks and behold, I Myself (God) am bringing floodwaters on the earth, to destroy from under heaven all flesh in which is the breath of life; everything that is on the earth shall die. But I will establish My covenant with you; and you shall go into the ark—you, your sons, your wife, and your sons' wives with you. And of every living thing of all flesh you shall bring two of every sort into the ark, to keep them alive with you; they shall be male and female. Of the birds after their kind, of animals after they're kind, and of every creeping thing of the earth after its kind, two of every kind will come to you to keep them alive. And you shall take for yourself of all food that is eaten, and you shall gather it to yourself; and it shall be food for you and for them." **Genesis 6:22 NKJ** Thus Noah did; according to all that God commanded him, so he did.

The Great Flood: Genesis 7:1-6 NKJ "Then Lord then said to Noah, "Go into the ark, you and your whole family, because I have found you righteous in this generation. Take with you seven pairs of every kind of clean animal, a male and its mate, and one pair of every kind of unclean animal, a male and its mate, and also seven pairs of every kind of bird, male and female, to keep their various kinds alive throughout the earth. Seven days from now I will send rain on the earth for forty days and forty nights, and I will wipe from the face of the earth every living creature I have made." And Noah did all that the Lord commanded him. Noah was six hundred years old when the floodwaters came on the earth. **Genesis 7:17-19 NKJ** Now the flood was on the earth forty days. The waters increased and lifted up the ark, and it rose high above the earth. The waters prevailed and greatly increased on the earth, and the ark moved about on the surface of the waters. And the waters prevailed exceedingly on the earth, and all the high hills under the whole heaven were covered. **Genesis 8:13-14 NKJ** And it came to pass in the six hundred and first year, in the first month, the first day of the month, that the waters were dried up from the earth; and Noah removed the covering of the ark and looked, and indeed the surface of the ground was dry. And in the second month, on the twenty-seventh day of the month, the earth was dried. **Genesis 9:1-3 NKJ** So God blessed Noah and his sons, and said to them: " Be fruitful and multiply, and fill the earth. And the fear of you and the dread of you shall be on every beast of the earth, on every bird of the air, on all that move on the earth, and on all the fish of the sea. They are given into your hand. Every moving thing that lives shall be food for you. I have given you all things, even as the green herbs. **Genesis 9:8-11 NKJ** "Then God spoke to Noah and to his sons with him, saying: "And as for Me, behold, I establish My covenant with you and with your descendants after you, and with every living creature that is with you: the birds, the cattle, and every beast of the earth with you, of all that go out of the ark, every beast of the earth. Thus I establish My covenant with you: Never again shall all flesh be cut off by the waters of the flood; never again shall there be a flood to destroy the earth."

The Promise: Genesis 9:12-17 NKJ "And God said: This is the sign of the covenant which I make between Me and you, and every living creature that is with you, for perpetual generations: I set My rainbow in the cloud, and it shall be for the sign of the covenant between Me and the earth. It shall be, when I bring a cloud over the earth, that the rainbow shall be seen in the cloud, and I will remember My covenant which is between Me and you and every living creature of all flesh; the waters shall never again become a flood to destroy all flesh. The rainbow shall be in the cloud, and I will look on it to remember the everlasting covenant between God and every living creature of all flesh that is on the earth." And God said to Noah, "This is the sign of the covenant which I have established between Me and all flesh that is on the earth." What an amazing gift God has given us: displaying

His presence, in the glory of a rainbow. God's word is written as an everlasting covenant for all humans. Our flesh is limited to eventual death; but as spirits, we who believe, have been given the pleasure of everlasting life in God's kingdom, to follow and honor His love for us.

The Scientific Explanation: A rainbow is a metrological phenomenon that is caused by reflection, refraction and dispersion of light in water droplets resulting in a spectrum of light appearing in the sky. It takes the form of a multicolored circular arc. Rainbows caused by sunlight, always appear in the section of sky directly opposite the sun. Rainbows can be full circles. However, the observer normally sees only an arc formed by illuminated droplets above the ground, and centered on a line from the sun to the observer's eye. In a primary rainbow, the arc shows red on the outer part and violet on the inner side. This rainbow is caused by light being when entering a droplet of water, then reflected inside on the back of the droplet and refracted again when leaving it.

The above definition is well done in scientific terms, but according to the Bible, it is by God's statement, indicating a phenomenon that claims His unique abilities, written a few thousand years ago, and are relevant today. God is reminding us of His presence! Occationaly we get the opportunity to admire this phenomenal gift, and and remember His promise. The most fascinating comparison to nature, is not defined by science alone, because the; who, what, why, when and where; cannot be completely defined without facts to account for description in all things. There are many presentations in science that cannot be proven in facts, but are only presented as theory. Historical change: It has been a long time since the day's of Noah. His surroundings were quite different, compared to now.

Jesus Himself claims: Matthew 6:34 NKJ " Therefore do not worry about tomorrow, for tomorrow will worry about its own things. Sufficient for the day is its own trouble." As we reflect on the historical process, many changes in the direction for 'all living things' appear to be going in the direction of progress. But what about us humans? Thinking about the progress in life it is interesting to glance at the industrial resolution, that began advancement toward the fast pace life we have today

Industrial Revolution: Eric Hobsbawm held that the Industrial Revolution began in Britain in the 1780s and was not fully felt until the 1830s or 1840s, while T. S. Ashton held that it occurred roughly between 1760 and 1830. (theory?)

Progress: Much has been gained since the industrial revolution, beginning with improvements from individual manual labor and farm labor, to a greater degree of industrialization based collective labor, during the first one hundred years in United States history. The Industrial Revolution occurred in two distinct phases: The First Industrial Revolution occurred during the latter part of the eighteenth century, through the first half of the nineteenth century, then the Second Industrial Revolution advanced following the Civil War . Among the main contributors to the First Industrial Revolution were Samual Slater's introduction of British Industrial methods in textile manufacturing to the United States, Eli Whitney's invention of the

Cotten gin. E .l du Pant's. in the second revolution, made improvements in chemistry and gunpowder making, industrial advancements necessitated by the War of 1812 , as well as the construction of the Erie Canal among other developments, were completed. (Wikipedia)

God's Gift to Mankind: Humans, are dominate in controlling habitats on earth, because of the intellect God gave us. Where does intellect come from? Some animals are very smart, but most rely on instinct to meet the requirements of their existence. What guides this source of instinct? Birds, insects, and plants, bring a balance to life, providing substance in the form of pollination, to grow and multiply the needed fuel for all living creatures. Is it by chance? Is it by intellect? Or from a power of a greater source…other than Humans? Why did God Create us in the first place? From the beginning, by the power of His love, God's character, including His supreme truth and justice, should be considered and trusted. God helps us find contentment in living. Loving others as He loves us, is the most essential part of our being. He created us to commune with him, as our supreme being, because He calls us, His children! God commands us to proclaim love, which is completely opposite from the destructive state of hate. The difficulty in following God's command, is the realistic presence He gives us in having free choice. In every interaction, we have a choice to respond in love, or pay the consequences of sin. Using self centered responses in our opinions, is not a sin, but using anything opposite of good intent, is characteristic of being sinful. It seems simple enough to love those who respond in love, but what happens when the one who rejects the intent of your love, and remarks with sarcastic comments? Are you motivated to sincerely love others from your heart? Are you using your love as a good thing to do? Do opinions come into play? What is the truth in your purpose share? Not one human is capable of loving others, as God Loves us! We must conclude; the life, death and resurrection of Jesus Christ, as both God and Man, reveals the intent of God's love, using His Son's sacrifice for our redemption.

Act of Remorse: When we recognize our misdeeds, usually with emotional moments, not reflecting our true self, we should take action to apologies. God leads us to repentance if our deeds are not in line with reconciliation and our sin is evident. **2 Corinthians 5:21 NKJ** " Now then, we are ambassadors for Christ, as though God was pleading through us, we implore you on Christ's behalf, be reconciled to God. For He made Him who knew no sin, to be sin for us, that we might become the righteousness of God in Him." By the Word of God's Son, we are able to understand the difference between love and hate, right or wrong, good or bad, leading to the conclusion that if we can believe the message brought to us by Jesus, and His sacrifice… it is the most powerful demonstration of love, leading us to also serve others, with love. **Colossians 2:6-10 NKJ** " As you therefore have received Christ Jesus the Lord, so walk in Him, rooted and built up in Him and established in the faith, as you have been taught, abounding in it with thanksgiving. Beware lest anyone cheat you through philosophy and empty deceit, according to the tradition of men, according to the basic principles of the world, and not according to Christ. For in Him dwells all the fullness of the Godhead bodily; and you are complete in Him, who is the head of all principality and power". Even though we 'can-not' achieve the level of love brought to us in Jesus, we can entrust our souls to follow His lead." Believing; as we believe, we are: Accepted in Christ, Secure in Christ, and most of all are… Significant in Christ. What does that mean?

Who I Am In Christ ... by Neil T. Anderson

Accepted:

John 1:12 But as many as received Him, to them He gave the right to become children of God, to those who believe in His name

John 15:15 John bore witness of Him and cried out, saying, "This was He of whom I said, 'He who comes after me is preferred before me, for He was before me.'"

Romans 5:1 Therefore, having been justified by faith, we have peace with God through our Lord Jesus Christ.

1 Corinthians 6:17 But he who is joined to the Lord is one spirit with Him.

1 Corinthians 6:20 For you were bought at a price; therefore glorify God in your body and in your spirit, which are God's.

1 Corinthians 12:27 Now you are the body of Christ, and members individually.

Ephesians 1:1 Paul, an apostle of Jesus Christ by the will of God, To the saints who are in Ephesus, and:

Ephesians 1:5 having predestined us to adoption as sons by Jesus Christ to Himself, according to the good pleasure of His will,

Ephesians 2:18 For through Him we both have access by one Spirit to the Father.

Colossians 1:14 in whom we have redemption through His blood, the forgiveness of sins.

Colossians 2:10 and you are complete in Him, who is the head of all principality and power.

Secure:

Romans 8: 1-2 There is therefore now no condemnation to those who are in Christ Jesus, who do not walk according to the flesh, but according to the Spirit. For the law of the Spirit of life in Christ Jesus has made me free from the law of sin and death.

Romans 8:28 And we know that all things work together for good to those who love God, to those who are the called according to His purpose.

Romans 8:33-34 Who shall bring a charge against God's elect? It is God who justifies. Who is he who condemns? It is Christ who died, and furthermore is also risen, who is even at the right hand of God, who also makes intercession for us.

Romans 8:35 Who shall separate us from the love of Christ? Shall tribulation, or distress, or persecution, or famine, or nakedness, or peril, or sword?

2 Corinthians 1:21 Now He who establishes us with you in Christ and has anointed us is God,

Colossians 3:3 For you died, and your life is hidden with Christ in God.

Philippians 1:6 being confident of this very thing, that He who has begun a good work in you will complete it until the day of Jesus Christ;

Philippians 3:20 For our citizenship is in heaven, from which we also eagerly wait for the Savior, the Lord Jesus Christ

2 Timothy 1:7 For God has not given us a spirit of fear, but of power and of love and of a sound mind.

Hebrews 4:16 Let us therefore come boldly to the throne of grace, that we may obtain mercy and find grace to help in time of need.

1 John 5:18 We know that whoever is born of God does not sin; but he who has been born of God keeps himself, and the wicked one does not touch him.

Significant:

Matthew 5:13-14 " You are the salt of the earth; but if the salt loses its flavor, how shall it be seasoned? It is then good for nothing but to be thrown out and trampled underfoot by men. You are the light of the world. A city that is set on a hill cannot be hidden."

John 15:1-5 " I am the true vine, and My Father is the vinedresser. I am the vine, you are the branches. He who abides in Me, and I in him, bears much fruit; for without Me you can do nothing."

John 15:16 You did not choose Me, but I chose you and appointed you that you should go and bear fruit, and that your fruit should remain, that whatever you ask the Father in My name He may give you.

Acts 1:8 But you shall receive power when the Holy Spirit has come upon you; and you shall be witnesses to Me in Jerusalem, and in all Judea and Samaria, and to the end of the earth."

1 Corinthians 3:16 Do you not know that you are the temple of God and that the Spirit of God dwells in you?

2 Corinthians 5:17-20 Therefore, if anyone is in Christ, he is a new creation; old things have passed away; behold, all things have become new. Now all things are of God, who has reconciled us to Himself through Jesus Christ, and has given us the ministry of reconciliation, that is, that God was in Christ reconciling the world to Himself, not imputing their trespasses to them, and has committed to us the word of reconciliation. Now then, we are ambassadors for Christ, as though God we're pleading through us: we implore you on Christ's behalf, be reconciled to God.

2 Corinthians 6:1 We then, as workers together with Him also plead with you not to receive the grace of God in vain.

Ephesians 2:6 and raised us up together, and made us sit together in the heavenly places in Christ Jesus,

Ephesians 2:10 For we are His workmanship, created in Christ Jesus for good works, which God prepared beforehand that we should walk in them.

Ephesians 3:12 in whom we have boldness and access with confidence through faith in Him.

Philippians 4:13 I can do all things through Christ who strengthens me.

Accolades: When I first read this powerful posting, I did not know who Neil was, but after reading his biography I am very aware he has blessed many of us through his efforts and his ministry. Revealing what love Christ has for all of us who believe. Surprised and grateful when I found 'Neil's work', simply constructed, with the most powerful message; he has given me confidence in my role as a believer. In Christ alone I take my stand! Thank you Neil for accepting the power of God working in your life and for the many contributions you have made to help us follow and commune with our Heavenly Father. We are not a meaningless creation, made by a disinterested character. God created us to have fellowship with Him , to share in His love. He is intensely interested in our lives, loving us beyond our comprehension, not because He must, but because He chooses us to be part of His existence, as we believe in His Son.

How hard is it to befriend God?

First: You have to believe He exists, proven by the documentation found in His word.

Second: Consideration of who He is, as supreme being;. " God is love." He gives us free choice to believe and follow Him, (avoiding any robotic interaction), to believe in Him or not.

Third: The power of sin in our flesh, can never please God, and we cannot battle it on our own. In his forbearance God left our sin unpunished, using animal sacrifice for repentance of our sin. Eventually, this method became redundant, without sincerity, failing to become one with God. Then... Jesus committed Himself to die in the flesh, to set us free from the judgement of our sins forever. As we believe in Him, we are set free from any judgement in our flesh.

Forth: Jesus came, setting aside His power from some elements in Heaven, Living as the only true 'God-man', with faultless innocence; Jesus consumed our sin, past, present and future, giving us opportunity to believe in Him, or be separated from God forever. As a choice! Jesus died to give purity to mankind as we believe in Him. We can consume His spiritual power as we believe and follow Him. We must remember to the depth of our souls... Jesus is our Savior!

A Passage To The Kingdom of Heaven: Revelation 21: 3-4 NKJ " And I heard a loud voice from heaven saying, Behold, the tabernacle of God is with men, and He will dwell with them, and they shall be His people. God Himself will be with them and be their God. And God will wipe away every tear from their eyes; there shall be no more death, nor sorrow, nor crying. There shall be no more pain, for the former things have passed away."

Befriending Eternal God: How do we compare to the wisdom of God? Dictionary , (noun):-Wisdom: The quality of having experience, knowledge, and good judgment; the quality of being wise: listen to his words of wisdom. Seek the soundness of an action or decision with regard to the application of experience, knowledge, and good judgment:

UNDERSTANDING WISDOM:

CHAPTER FOUR

King Solomon: One of many favorite stories in the Bible, is the life of King Solomon. All wisdom belongs to God, and mankind only receives what God gives him. In the case of Solomon, He was young when he met God, and immature in leading the kingdom of David. As a youngster he knew and loved God. In the beginning of his reign, he asked God for wisdom to understand his commission. God is all knowing, new the outcome of Solomons action.; Claiming from the beginning, Solomon would be the first and the last in the flesh of man having wisdom in all areas of thought. **1 Kings 1:32-35 NKJ** " And King David said, Call to me Zadok the priest, Nathan the prophet, and Benaiah the son of Jehoiada." So they came before the king. The king also said to them, "Take with you the servants of your lord, and have Solomon my son ride on my own mule, and take him down to Gihon, there let Zadok the priest and Nathan the prophet anoint him king over Israel; and blow the horn, and say, 'Long live King Solomon!' Then you shall come up after him, and he shall come and sit on my throne, and he shall be king in my place. For I have appointed him to be ruler over Israel and Judah." **Wisdom given to Solomon**: **1 Kings 3:5-12 NKJ** "At Gibeon the Lord appeared to Solomon in a dream by night; and God said, Ask! What shall I give you? And Solomon said: You have shown great mercy to Your servant David my father, because he walked before You in truth, in righteousness, and in uprightness of heart with You; You have continued this great kindness for him, and You have given him a son to sit on his throne, as it is this day. Now, O' Lord my God, You have made Your servant king instead of my father David, but I am a little child; I do not know how to go out or come in. And Your servant is in the midst of Your people whom You have chosen, a great people, too numerous to be numbered or counted. Therefore give to Your servant an understanding heart to judge Your people, that I may discern between good and evil. For who is able to judge this great people of Yours? The speech pleased the Lord, that Solomon had asked this thing. Then God said to him: because you have asked this thing, and have not asked long because life for yourself, nor have asked riches for yourself, nor have asked the life of your enemies, but have asked for yourself understanding to discern justice, behold, I have done according to your words; see…" I have given you a wise and understanding heart, so that there has not been anyone like you before you, nor shall any like you arise after you. And I have also given you what you have not asked: both riches and honor, so that there shall not be anyone like you among the kings all your days." **1 Kings 9:4-5 NKJ** "Now if you walk before Me as your father David walked, in integrity of heart and in uprightness, to do according to all that I have commanded you, and if you keep My statutes and My judgments, then I will establish the throne of your kingdom over Israel forever, as I promised. -**Kings 9:6-9 NKJ** "But if you or your sons at all turn from following Me, and do not keep My commandments and My statutes which I have set before you, but go and serve other gods and worship them, then I will cut off Israel from the land which I have given them; and this house which I have consecrated for My name, I will cast out of

My sight. Israel will be a proverb and a byword among all peoples. And as for this house, which is exalted, everyone who passes by it will be astonished and will hiss, and say, 'Why has the Lord done thus to this land and to this house?' Then they will answer, 'Because they forsook the Lord their God, who brought their fathers out of the land of Egypt, and have embraced other gods, and worshiped them and served them; therefore the Lord has brought all this calamity on them.' "

Solomon's HeartTurns from the Lord: 1 Kings 11:1-4 NKJ " But King Solomon loved many foreign women, as well as the daughter of Pharaoh: women of the Moabites, Ammonites, Edomites, Sidonians, and Hittites— from the nations of whom the Lord had said to the children of Israel, " You shall not intermarry with them, nor they with you. Surely they will turn away your hearts after their gods." "Solomon clung to these in love. And he had seven hundred wives, princesses, and three hundred concubines; and his wives turned away his heart. For it was so, when Solomon was old, that his wives turned his heart after other gods; and his heart was not loyal to the Lord his God, as was the heart of his father David."

Death of Solomon:

2 Chronicles 9:29-31 NKJ Solomon reigned in Jerusalem over all Israel forty years. Then Solomon rested with his fathers, and was buried in the City of David with his father. And Rehoboam his son reigned in his place". Solomon left us an account of the futility of life, without trusting in God. How sad this is, the end of his Devine wisdom, given to him for good counsel, that eventually lead to failure, living in the flesh, as God predicted.

Ecclesiastes 1:15-18 NKJ Solomon writes: " What is crooked cannot be made straight, And what is lacking cannot be numbered. I communed with my heart, saying, Look, I have attained greatness, and have gained more wisdom than all who were before me in Jerusalem. My heart has understood great wisdom and knowledge. And I set my heart to know wisdom and to know madness and folly. I perceive that this also is grasping for the wind. For in much wisdom is much grief, And he who increases knowledge, increases sorrow". It is sad for me to think that Solomon, started out with wisdom and a pure heart, then fell to a pitiful way of life in the end. The power of the flesh is weak, without the protection of God's Spirit. Becoming indignant, Solomons choice at the end of his life, reminded us of what God said. **1 Kings 3:12 NKJ** " I have given you a wise and understanding heart, so that there has not been anyone like you before you, nor shall any like you arise after you." God knew Solomon's fate from the beginning. As He does all of us who believe or not. When we believe and follow, we will eventually walk in God's kingdom, and be judged by our faith, or condemned by not believing in God's saving grace… **"Jesus!."** Thank God for His Mercy and Grace! Freeing us from the punishment of sin, we can not resolve, as we commune with our Savior, Jesus Christ; we are free.

Kingdoms? Was Solomon's kingdom among the longest lasting in History? What are the longest-lasting empires, governments, or nations? The world has seen some exceptionally successful societies and empires. The following are some of the longest-lasting governments and nations in world history. Analyzing which governments in history, have lasted the longest amount of time, the answer, might be different than you expect.

Does a nation get disqualified for being occupied by a foreign power for a time? What if a nation joins together with another, like in the case of the United Kingdom, or the United States? What about cultures that have never formed a formal state or nation? How does the United States compare to other long-lived nations? Some of the longest-lasting governments and nations in world history are recorded.

Recorded Empires:

- **The Pandya Empire** (1850 years)

  This society of Southern India is considered the longest-lasting empire in history. It dominated trade and was extremely wealthy due to agriculture and control of fisheries and pearl beds. A series of kings ruled the region during this period, which lasted from about 500 BC to 1350 AD.

- **Byzantine Empire** (1123 years)

  Also known as the Eastern Roman Empire, the Byzantine culture based in Constantinople (now Istanbul) dominated much of Europe and the Levant . By the 13th century, the empire was in decline, and although it was re-established in 1261, it was never a major power. The empire was finally overthrown by the Ottoman Turks in 1453.

- **Silla** (992 years)

  This kingdom, originally established in 57 BC, eventually covered much of the Korean peninsula. By 527, Silla was officially a Buddhist nation—although this did not discourage its frequent wars with the other Korean kingdoms. Nevertheless, the nation enters history as one of the oldest of all time.

- **Ethiopian Empire** (837 years)

  One of the few African nations to hold out against European colonialism, the Ethiopian Empire (also known as Abyssinia) asted from 1137 until 1975 (it may have continued, but the government was overthrown in a coup). Multiple European nations (including Italy and Britain) attempted to colonize

Ethiopia during the late 1800's, but were defeated by Ethiopian forces.

- **Roman Empire** (1000 years)

The classic Roman Empire that we know most about, the society that was based on Rome and counted Julius Caesar among its first rulers, lasted for nearly 500 years. This followed the period of the Roman Republic, which also lasted nearly 500 years, but civil war and instability led to the dissolution of the Senate and the founding of the Empire. At the end of its life, in the 5th century, Rome began to collapse under the weight of invasions, and eventually broke up. After 450 years as a republic, Rome became an empire in the wake of Julius Caesar's rise and fall in the first century B.C. The long and triumphant reign of its first emperor, Augustus, began a golden age of peace and prosperity; by contrast, the Roman Empire's decline and fall by the fifth century A.D.

- **San Marino** (415+ years)

Perhaps the oldest government still in operation today, more or less unchanged, is the Italian micro-state of San Marino. With a land area of less than 30 square miles, the nation has been able to maintain its boundaries and integrity of government for more than 400 years.

- **Aboriginal Australian Cultures** (50,000 years)

This is a special case, since aboriginal Australians have never formed empires or states in the same sense as the other known nations. But it is believed that Aboriginal culture has remained intact, with largely continuous religious and political structure, for more than 50,000 years.

Compared to these empires, we have a long way to go! As of 2020, the United States has been a nation 244years: Since the Declaration of Independence in 1776, that seems like a long time, but only producing a few generations, compared to the other cultures and governments listed above. The rise and fall of our Nation is questionable. As we consider the extreme difference in the formation of our country... does it have the same patriotic principals as our Founding Fathers? If not... how it has it changed? Why include history of Empires in this presentation?

The Bible, has many translations to a truthful message without alterations. It speaks about spiritual events through out History. Actual recordings of world history, and the presences of a Devine Creator is available, to compare how Empires who dominated its inhabitants for a period of time, eventually became obsolete.

Roman Empire Vs. The United States

Choosing a comparison of the Roman Empire to the United States of America, the intent is to consider powerful nations, and what might lead to our demise. Rome was able to gain its empire in large part, by extending some form of citizenship to many of the people it conquered. Military expansion drove economic development, bringing enslaved people and back to Rome, which in turn transformed the city of Rome and Roman culture.

How did the Roman Empire, fail?

During the early republic, the Roman State grew exponentially in both size and power. Rome's complex political institutions, however, began to crumble under the weight of the growing empire, ushering in an era of turmoil and violence. Does that Sound familiar to our country today? Invasions of Barbarian tribes, reveals the most straight-forward theory for Western Rome's collapse. The fall on a string of military losses sustained against outside forces. Rome had tangled with Germanic tribes for centuries, but by the 300's "barbarian" groups like the Goths had encroached beyond the Empire's borders.

Eight reasons why Rome Fell: 1) Invasions by Barbarian tribes., 2) Economic troubles and over reliance on slave labor, 3) The rise of the Eastern Empire. 4) Over expansion and military overspending. 5) Government corruption and political instability. 6) The arrival of the Huns and the migration of the Barbarian tribes. 7) Christianity and the loss of traditional values. 8) Weakening of the Roman legions. In comparison, it doesn't take a genius to see the resemblance of how our nation is changing.? The above, 5, 7, 8, are evident in our country at this very moment; It is a big worry for our future! (https:www.history.com/news)

Matthew 24:6 NKJ " And you will hear of wars and rumors of wars. See that you are not troubled; for all these things must come to pass, but the end is not yet." During the past decades, changes in each generation is encouraging us to lead a different of way of life, as we progress toward the future; avoiding our founding fathers is a big mistake; if we don't get our unity together and pay attention to the Constitution!

CHANGING TIMES:
CHAPTER FIVE

Penning my schoolwork while growing up, in the forties and fifties, I hoped for a manual typewriter too better my penmanship and find a better way to spell correctly. I used dictionaries and book references, to make my way through the educational system. Today: the toys we have, are guiding us to a faster way of life, while learning in a shorter period of time, often without scrutiny. We are smothered with an influence that seems to draw us away from reality; giving opportunity of exposure and control by others? Social media is fun to use, and gives a quick look at interesting topics, but what about those interrupting clips we are bombarded with? We often overlook flaws, to keep on track with what we are currently involved with. How do we determine if our privacy, is intact or if we are bing bombard with subliminal brain washing? Does social media and high tech companies have control of our lives? Is our political system working for us, or against us? Who is responsible for all the Kaos we experience? How can we maintain freedom and be at peace? Is the mainstream news presenting a complete truthful picture of their topics, or printing only one side of the story as lies.? Is our voting system safe and accurate? In the political realm, how did they come to slandering others, as their first choice, instead of nurturing our free country by, interaction and compromise? Why aren't they moving in a way, to consider both sides to the tasks at hand? Can we as individuals do anything about these conditions? Are we out of our control? Who has the power to control our lives? Is it called freedom, or suppression? Who has our best interest at heart, mankind or God? Stop for a moment, put away your toys! Find a private place to be alone. With the intent of evaluating your life. Use your brain to conclude if you have a valuable reference and preferences to depend on… one you can use for your safety! Does the future look promising, or questionable? What is the most valuable reference controlling your contentment? What does your world look like? Does it appear satisfying? What are three things that make you satisfied? If not satisfied, can you identify the reason for not being satisfied? Do you try to ignore it? Is there more than one thing, leading to your dissatisfaction? How do you proceed when change effects your life?

1 Corinthians 1:28 b-31 NKJ " God has chosen, and the things which are not to bring to nothing the things that are, that no flesh should glory in His presence. But of Him you are in Christ Jesus, who became for us wisdom from God—and righteousness and sanctification and redemption that, as it is written; "He who glories, let him glory in the Lord."

John 6:63-65 NKJ " It is the Spirit who gives life; the flesh profits nothing. The words that I speak to you are spirit, and they are life." No flesh should glory in His presence! God has provided me life in His existence; what I do with this life… is my choice! Praise God for bringing His Glory to my attention. Throughout my life, I faltered without His presence. Now truly believing that sin is anything that stands between me and my relationship with God. I reconcile to the Father daily, thanking Jesus for his absolute commitment to bring anyone to His kingdom, who understands His love. Repenting: Is a daily routine. Jesus has set me free, to commune with 'Our Father' about anything!

The Holy Spirit comforts me, allowing me freedom to recognize the sin in my flesh …that is never ending. Take time to commune with God. This is a cohesive way of speaking the truth, from our heart, as it strengthens faith in God. Believing and honoring His love and forgiveness, by acknowledge both good and bad, confessing to His power and presence, is the gift of redemption. There is no glory in my name, but God's Glory in God's Creation; is Evident! As we honor Him, and His Son, using Holy Spirit to guide us. God's intent, is to expresses love beyond our knowledge., using the Holy Spirit, known as counselor, to interpret our thoughts and prayers, as He communes to God for reference, in His Will. Having faith, we can avoid many mistakes in choice, as the Spirit within us guides us toward a better direction to follow.

Faith in God: As we follow God's precepts, the difference between good and evil, are polar opposite! Submitting to the love of Jesus our savior, allows the great journey toward eternity, without punishment of our sin. It magnificently solidifies, the God of the Bible, is the living and loving; Great… " I AM. " There is no other! Along with good and evil; pain and suffering are two elements we battle often. Many throughout the world, are challenged to find a way to cope with difficulties. The 'why' of this situation is not relevant; but the how… is learning to cope, then work to find a satisfactory outcome, which demands personal effort, sometimes exhausting, toward a goal of compromise., leading to stability and satisfaction. The Goal of stability, is complete when nothing else needs to be done, having acceptance to whatever is left.

Considering Life Changes: Becoming entangled with irreversible changes, physically or mentally, demands a new way of experiencing, altered daily routines. Changes can be temporary, or permanent. Most do not consider difficult challenges in life, until they happen. Some born with abnormal limitations, do not consider what could have been, but demonstrate the ability to live with what they have, as a unique person. Pain and suffering are not qualities of a happy life. It is my intention to expose the difficulty in altering physical or emotional state of mind, adapting to a new way of activity. After understanding and accepting any loss, your instinct toward acceptance will lead you to perseverance, motivation and compromise. Routines begin with a slow pace, challenging adjustment to daily living. In the beginning of rehabilitation, it is important to find encouragement by using uplifting thoughts. Your demeanor is best, at a positive level. Humor is often used as a diversion to uncomfortable needed routines. The important thing to remember is to find something that detours negative thoughts. One of my favorite Television programs is found on KSPS channel 107, Spokane Washington, it is called 'Nature'.

Each program focuses on the balance of life, in a verity of living creatures, demonstrating the power of creation and the balance we need to maintain life. It is uplifting to see the beauty in nature, exposing the balance of inhabitants throughout the world. However, it is difficult to watch how life is snuffed out, for the greater good, as the habitats of nature attempt to thrive, but are doomed by their enemies.

Many of us enjoy outdoor recreation, removing ourselves from fast pace living to relax away from daily responsibilities. Enjoyment can bring long term memories of good times to share, or as diversion in uncomfortable times. When we face difficult change, battling and adjusting to an unwanted direction, gets extremely personal, leading us to find compromise in our discomfort as soon as possible. One enemy to avoid is self pity. Considering all creatures in the world, our intellect seems to control life as we know it. Our talents, abilities, and power, not only have jurisdiction over the creatures on earth, but we also have the capacity to compromise, when faced with changing events. Depending on the circumstances, these events, good or bad, will result in change, in the choices we make. Resolutions can be complicated over time, using compromise with satisfaction, to conclude the right direction. For me, God is the answer to the "why we are here." As we suffer, God is able to give direction and comfort as we rely on Him to lead us forward in spirit. What happens next is up to us. The end game of our life, as we believe in Him; he will welcome us in His kingdom, without suffering and pain; But for now we are flesh in the spirit that needs to find resources for our well being.

The Future? Throughout the working period of our lives, we may or may not take time to plan for the future. Why? Because most of us seem to live in the here and now. Here's the thing… I too am living in the here and now, but at the age of seventy-nine. So what is the difference between you and me? I have no opportunity to regroup and provide income for my needs. I cannot change the direction of my deteriorating body, as time is running out. My emotions are centered to function as best I can. Hoping to interact with my family until the end. Most of all… I do not want to leave a burden to my family or others, by having unresolved debt. Many of us do not have the opportunity to save for the future. The important thing is to plan on how you will manage to survive! Social security is not enough, welfare is not enough, living with other family members might be a solution, but it is not guaranteed. The dilemma of maintaining good quality of life, after leaving the work force, all depends on how we had planed for the future? Have you noticed any elderly workers beyond retirement age, working for small wages? They probably need the income to survive. Whether we accumulate things or not, depends on the circumstances of how we choose to live our life. Not everyone is successful maintaining financial independence and many suffer in life because of their bad choices.

According to the dictionary: 'Choice' as a noun is: an act of selecting or making a decision when faced with two or more possibilities: (the choice between good and evil.) A course of action, thing, or person that is selected or decided upon: (this CD drive is the perfect choice for your computer) . (Is God real? Is God a perfect choice to believe in?) A range of possibilities from which one or more may be selected: (you can have a sofa made to order in a choice of over forty fabrics). . However, only one of two choices in life will decide your fate for the future…Believe in God or not! There is always a choice, good or bad, right or wrong, love or hate, believe or do not believe… we are free to choose a direction to follow. The definition of choice from the above, provides a range of possibilities. How we chose our own destiny is within our human rights. However, our human capability and personal choices are highly influenced by the environment we live in. Some choose and follow their own choices as free agents, others are oppressed and limited in choice; having no hope of becoming independent or free. Still others rely on personal faith, seeking a god of their liking. Faith by itself is useless, but when we consider and believe in Jesus, we are justified as righteous in His name. Without believing… we are on our own! Designated to have ever lasting life in Heaven., Jesus is the strength to all believers, as our Lord and Savior, and our future… choose Him or not.

Tolerating Choice: The remedy to physical and emotional changes, test the afflicted to seek a level of stability, using self examination. Accepting the current condition is the immediate response toward recovery. Adjusting to an altering capacity, focusing on 'goals', to help toward recovery, is essential. The response to change, rests on the 'individual', experiencing the need to seek a satisfactory resolution. Tolerance is the ability or willingness to exist as is, accepting what is available to compromise for a new way of living, over a long period of time.Opinions or resolutions from others, do not always benefit the recipient. The one who is adjusting to change, is seeking a pathway of acceptance. There are many scenarios in reaching a compromise, but the most important one … 'is yours'! We must remember compromise is not a true solution, only a temporary fix.. Why is that? Everything in life is a choice. How you choose your future, is up to you. Many bad choices will leave you in despair, but the good ones, lead to peace and satisfaction. For me; there is only one good choice that towers above all choice: to accept or reject the God of the Bible. Refusing, or denying the sacrifice of His Son for our redemption, is a mistake leading us to everlasting torment, in the power of darkness. When my wife, asked her father on his death bed, do you know Jesus? At the age of 92, he said; "I have to know him, he is the only way out of here." Not knowing if he truly accepted Jesus, this remark spoke volumes in his faith. Living a long life, should not be our biggest concern. Living a life that is content at any age, should be what we strive for.

Family History: My father-in-law grew up on a small farm, surrounded by a pleasant peaceful environment. As a child, he had some chores to do each day, helping the family live and survive. When older, he worked in the apple business until he became a manager at one of the storage processing plants. He returned there, after working for the Boeing Aircraft Company during World War Two. After the war, he was able to build a two bedroom house, and settled down on a nine acre plot, given to him by his father. Later He added a third bedroom to keep his two kids from arguing the usual sibling counter attacks; needing to separate them to their own space. For me, as a kid from California, growing up in the city, the serene atmosphere of peace and beauty in this farm setting, calmed my anxious soul. During the relaxing times, sitting next to Dad in the shade of a big fur tree, we were listening to the women sharing stories. Suddenly Dad lifted his hand, turning his wrist upward as if to stop something? As a dragon fly headed for his palm, then suddenly lifted up, like a helicopter, to avoid the blockage, then continued flying higher than Dad's fingers as he moved on. Llaughing out loud, considering what just happened? A simple pattern of life, relating to nature, inspired me to strive for the same demeanor, playing in the existence of God's Creation.

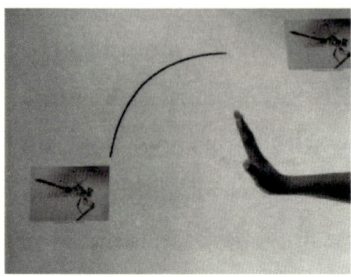

Consider the dragon fly: "The dragonfly, in almost every part of the world, symbolizes change, and change in the perspective of self realization. The kind of change that has its source in mental and emotional maturity and the understanding of the deeper meaning of life." Wow, perspective self realization? A kind of change involving mental and emotional maturity? Understanding in the deeper meaning of life? Isn't this thing, just a bug?

Considering this definition, and my father-in-law's statement about Jesus, the Dragonfly (playing the roll of the devil), is interrupted by Dad's stopping hand

(illustrating the roll of Jesus, keep us away from evil). It may in some way, demonstrate the power of our Lord, to avoid sin and protect us from evil. Bearing in mind the presence of sin in my life, the above illustration, cannot remove all of my sin. If this was true, it would probably lead me to surgery, because of the effects over taxing my wrist movement. In reality Jesus has removed my debts from sin, as I truly believe in Him. Also, how silly would it be, while out in public, as you observe several people trying to brush away their sin? What is the answer to avoid this dilemma?

Praying is the essence of the Christian life. Why? Jesus Himself, being Christ and man, demonstrated the power of prayer, essential to power found in Kingdom of Heaven, He has motivated us to peace and love, to everyone who believes, in Him. -**1 Timothy 4:4-5 NKJ** " For every creature of God is good, and nothing is to be refused, if it is received with thanksgiving; for it is sanctified by the word of God and prayer." Believing in shed blood of Jesus Christ, and His Saving Grace, we are justified in overcoming the punishment of all sin. Jesus claims us through His righteousness, by believing in Him, we have direct contact to the Father, enabling us to pray directly to Him, with a childlike mind. Prayers to the Father, are essential in the importance of staying in contact with our Creator. Jesus is perfect, without fault, and part of the triune God. Praying to the Father to intercede in times of trouble; praying for others; and prayers of reconciliation; are a few prayers, bonding us to believe God, will prevail ! However, we also must remember God is always present, wanting us to commune with Him on a daily bases. Jesus sets the example in the importance of communicating to the Father, as we stand fast in His will. Prayer is essential to maintain our connection to God, without ceasing. We must recognize our sins and account for them by reconciliation, to God in prayer. There is a difference in God's way, compared to our position in this world. The battle of good vs evil will continue to influence our daily routines. We must recognize our faults, asking for forgiveness and guidance, through His Holy Spirit. Sadly, recognition of sin, is diminishing, to an evil substandard of living; allowing freedom of choice in body and spirit, to do whatever we want. Why? Evil is slowly taking away our ability to love others as God loves us! God wants me to trust in His will, not mine. The power of God helps me recognize the need to repent from my fleshly ways, then strive for goodness, as

He uses the holy Spirit within me, to remain in faith… until I am with Him in heaven.!

Bonding with our Creator in prayer good or bad, is essential in receiving His blessing in all circumstances. Believing in the life, death and resurrection of Jesus, we are set free from condemnation for our sin. All of mankind must recognize the power of sin as forgiveness is through Jesus Christ. The penalty of our sin is removed as we confess, believe, and follow His will; If not we will be in darkness forever.

Self-Evaluation: Have you ever removed yourself from the routines of life, to consider the effect you have in those around you? How are we viewed in our daily interaction, according self or others? What does the input of others mean to us? How does their interaction effect our demeanor? What is the key element in being socially responsible? When questioned, we sometimes try to avoid a truthful response, because the truth may jeopardize a relationship we want to keep. Our desire to be loved, is to avoid hurting others. Also, conversations with intent of giving advice or support, can be misinterpreted, leading to conflict, and a probable need for reconciliation. So what is the solution in being myself? One thing I seldom do is, evaluate myself before I speak. The constant interruption from my lips, continues to take over other conversations in progress, getting a discouraged look from those I just interrupted. Through self evaluation, I figure my input was going to be brief, or something good to share, but ignored the respect of waiting for them to finish. Having minimal control of my actions, l often use power of reconciliation, hoping to be forgiven for any wrongdoing. A brief form of discretion, before conversations and discussions, should be at the forefront of my mind, to avoid inappropriate conflicts. The collective value in my discussions, fail to comprehend, without discretion. Discretion: noun; The quality of behaving or speaking in such a way as to avoid causing offense or revealing private information:

The freedom to decide what should be done in a particular situation… but life go's on to who I am as an interrupting babbler. When my family or friends see me approaching, they ignore me and keep talking, attempting to divert my interruption, as a bad habit. Years ago, my boss while, introducing me said …. "He will talk to you until you walk away." Self-evaluation can lead to difficult times. As I review the flaws in our personality. Compromising faults, brings hope for change, But, until I reach the comfort of heaven, my reconciliation era will never end as a babbler. Why? Because we will connect to the loving power and beauty in God's eternal heaven, without blame or sorrow, free from offending others, by following the laws of God's will. Self-evaluation is a heavy burden to many who are experiencing a tragic or difficult change, even when seeking accurate support from professionals. The key in overcoming a tragic event, is to accept the things you cannot change, then press froward to find a satisfactory level of tolerance, to live as best you can.

Do Not Worry: Matthew 6:25 NKJ " Therefore I say to you, do not worry about your life, what you will eat or what you will drink; nor about your body, what you will put on. Is not life more than food and the body more than clothing?" Difficult change in our lives, will require ability to adjust to new circumstances. Paramount for us, is to be satisfied with the outcome. Developing positive faith, contemplating what you have left, is far better than the negative reaction of, 'why me'? It Is very important to overcome small battles of recovery, before you can move on.

Hebrews 11:1-3, 11:6 NKJ " Now faith is the substance of things hoped for, the evidence of things not seen. For bye it, the elders obtained a good testimony. By faith we understand that the worlds were framed by the word of God, so that the things which are seen were not made of things which are visible. Without faith, it is impossible to please Him, for he who comes to God must believe that He is, and He is a rewarder of those who diligently seek Him." Faith fuels our ability, to do the best we can, with what we have. Physical or mental difficulties are not easy to overcome, so we must rely on available resources to help us regain a satisfactory way of living. **Romans 1:16-17 NKJ:** " For I am not ashamed of the gospel of Christ, for it is the power of God to salvation, for everyone who believes, for the Jew first and also for the Greek. For in it, the righteousness of God is revealed from faith to faith; as it is written, The just shall live by faith." What does 'the just' mean? An adjective: based on or behaving according to what is morally right and fair; a just and democratic society. Our union with God, does not happen by chance. Each one of us has to make a choice to believe in Him or not. The simplicity of this choice is a commitment to a source of love that brings peace, to understand to our existence. God says we are justified by believing the name Jesus Christ. God wants us to acknowledge Him; to develop a trusting personal relationship with Him; then live in peace and freedom using His precepts of grace, and guidance, but most of all…love. Unconditional love from our Creator is forever present. He asks nothing from us, but to acknowledge Him and follow His standard of love. He wants us to love others as he loves us. By believing, you begin a fascinating journey in understanding what this life is all about, then also receive the everlasting life to come.

Living in freedom or under oppression, you have one thing that cannot be taken from you…the choice of seeking the Spirit from God, living within you! We are unique within ourselves. The environment is given by God. The choices we make, within our beliefs or needs, are based on how to find satisfaction and peace. The God of the Holy Bible, is my choice to investigate the possibility of His existence, and find peace in my soul. During the first four decades of my life, I believed in a man called Jesus, who is God. He is the center of the Christian faith. At ten years old, not fully comprehending the significance of this process, I was baptized. However; God did not give me the Holy Spirit to guide me throughout my early life. At the age of ten, self indulgence trapped me, as I set goals for the future. During the first Thirty Six Years of my life, I believed in the God of the Bible, but had no idea in the powerful the gift of the Holy Spirit, who is dedicated to all believers who claim Jesus as their Savior, guiding us to follow God's Will Baptism symbolizes the death, burial and resurrection of Jesus, but it is not a guarantee to receive God's Holy Spirit, which guides us in our relationship with Him. Baptism is a form to acknowledge Jesus as our savior, symbolizing His life, death and resurrection. The true commitment to God, is receiving His Holy Spirit to guide us as we commit our honest belief in Jesus, from our souls. When we commit to the saving Grace of Jesus, truthfully from our heart and sole, He gives us the holy Spirit (the third part of our triune God) to receive knowledge and guidance helping us follow God's plan in true faith, receiving hoped peace.

I had no idea that " God's Holy Spirit" was needed to follow and commune with Him. As a believer in the life of Jesus, unfortunately, my early faith was weakened, subjected to worldly influence in what I can see, using World standards.; that eventually led me to the darkest moment of my life. Reaching the lowest period of my life… alone in my troubles, God seemed to be my only choice for help. Surprisingly, during the moment of tearful interaction, God changed my direction, and filled me with His Holy Spirit, because of my lack of faith in the first three decades of life, I needed the revival, and the power of Jesus to capture the missing part of my faith, and my earthly life. This change was subtle, but powerful enough to receive new guidance toward God's work, for the remainder of my life.. After a few adjustments to put God first, I began to seek God's presence. Now completely committed to

God, I commune with through the Holy Spirit throughout my day, in an attempt to honor and Love God as He loves me.

Holy Spirit: An essential part of getting to Heaven, is to receive Jesus as your Savior, then be guided by the Holy Spirit, as you place your complete faith in God's presence., Most of all, recognizing His tremendous love for us, and the beauty of His Majesty, revealing Salvation through His Son, as we believe and follow His Word. The Holy Spirit (third part of our triune God) knows if our faith is real, or not. We Humans are both flesh and spirit. When we die, our spirit returns too God to be judged for our sin (if not committed to Jesus). All who are committed to serving God, following His precepts, will be a reward for our servant's heart as we share the gift of life beyond; that Jesus. has given us. We all share both good and evil, committing to Jesus, battle is to save us for the good. The key trusting who rules, is given by our Spirit. Do we follow God with truth and love, committed to prayer, truly believing in Jesus? Or do we disregard Him, by committing or souls toward self-indulgence; by free choice in the power of worldly influence, caused by the devil, satin ?

The Power of Prayer: When contacting God in prayer, there are three answers to consider: Prayers; of Yes; excites praise to God for His resolution. Prayers of No: Means the alternative will make things worse than the current situation, or may last awhile, or even longer, toward resolution. Prayers of Wait: is the most difficult, Why? It is God's waiting period. Based in His Timing; He encouraging us to trust our faith in Him. for His Will to be done… not ours. If we maintain our true belief in Him., knowing the future is everlasting life in Heaven, it is enough for me to understand His Will is for the good. Prolonged repeated prayer about the same issue is challenging. Unanswered prayer can be tossed aside early, by the act of redundancy. This is Incorporated repetition frequently reminds us, of our need for a quick answer. Commitment to prolonged repeated prayer, is to let God know, we trust in His loving will. He guides our path. toward Heaven,. soon be with Him forever. Meanwhile our plea of prayer continues on in faith, focusing on Gods power save us for His good purpose. For me there is much satisfaction written in Biblical for us to understand the many situations connecting to God in Prayer.

After receiving the Holy Spirit to connect me to God's presence, my attempt to pray without ceasing is common in every day thoughts.. I can commune and trust God throughout the day, revealing His presence is always with me, using His Timing not mine Example: A lady in our church, needed prayer for relief of painful headaches that were medically unresolved, causing continued pain and suffering. As we gathered in our church, praying, for God to intervene, in all sorts of requests, we prayed for weeks to get positive results for our friend until she moved away. A few months later she contacted us, writing letter of praise!. The medical team cured her problem. This news uplifted our souls to know; God hears our prayers and answers them in His timing. But know this…God's timing is equated in Heavens time:

A Day in Heaven is like a Thousand Years on earth: 2 Peter 3:8 NKJ "But, Beloved, do not forget this one thing… that with the Lord one day is as a thousand years, and a thousand years as one day." Fascinated by a day in Heaven being a thousand years; doing the math…one deep breath, about three to four seconds on this planet, compares to about nineteen earth days, in Heavens time. At this speed, God knows things long before eve ask.

None of us are excluded from suffering and pain, and none of us can explain the reason for it. God's will, is for us to draw nearer to Him, and trust in His guidance. Jesus endured a tremendous example of pain and suffering. Being both God and man, in the Spirit and flesh.

His physical suffering and pain, was brutal, but He coped to the end; giving new life for others to follow in His loving example.

Comparing our time to heavens time: Comparing mankind to earth time, Jesus lived here about thirty-three years. However, when we calculate heavens time to one earth days; the time of Jesus as God/man on earth, was **less than an hour** in heavens time. As I play with this thought, time doesn't matter, when you live for eternity! Those of us who submit to the love of Jesus, understand His power and loving promise that He will never leave you or forsake you. **Hebrews 13:5 NKJ** " Let your conduct be without covetousness; be content with such things as you have. For He Himself has said, I will never leave you nor forsake you."

1 Peter 4:1-2 NKJ "Therefore, since Christ suffered for us in the flesh, arm yourselves also with the same mind, for He who has suffered in the flesh has ceased from sin, that He no longer should live the rest of His time in the flesh, for the lusts of men…but for the will of God." Making choices on our own, or praying to God for guidance, when pain and suffering occurs, leads to success or failure. Suffering is personal, to both believers and non-believers. Why is that? Anyone who is suffering, praying to God or not, must adjust to circumstances out of their control. Even those who have faith in God, attempt to overcome sadness, suffering and pain, like anyone else. Why do we suffer? Some seek to find the reason behind change, often capturing additional worry, adding to their anxiety. Many are challenged by the severity of the suffering, and give up completely. This struggle, caused by life altering change, has no specific recovery or outcome to follow. As individuals experiencing the event, they must provide their own adjustments that are satisfactory for them, then accept the change as best they can, moving on to acclimate a compromised outcome.

The Book of Job: In the Bible, the book of Job describes a man who honored God and pleased Him by his faith. This story tells us how God allowed 'Satan' to test Job with pain and suffering, to demonstrate his faithfulness. As a rich man, with a large family, Job lost everything, including the lives of his family, then also suffered physical pain as well, without response from God. As you read the account of this challenge, you will find others trying to figure out why this happened. They gave their reasons and suggestions, failing to console Job, who stood fast in his faith. During this process Job alienated his friends, turning to God only, seeking the reason why he was suffering.? Eventually the end result was a test of faith Job, pleased God, for his commitment of faith. After a few adjustments in his faithful reaction, God restored Job to greater riches and family than he had before. As Job discovered, it was a test of his loyalty and commitment to God, he also realized a need for repentance to God, for some of his reactions during the time of his trial.

My thoughts turn to the family he had before his test? It reminds me; when God takes away, He provides resolution, and Job's pervious family is with God in paradise.

Devine Suffering: Think of Jesus, suffering on the cross, how much He endured in agony reconciling us, to God The Father. consuming the judgement of our sin. His death presented the enrichment of his love, as an innocent and pure Surpreme Being. Jesus has given us opportunity to return and live in paradise forever. The simplicity of acknowledging Jesus and trusting in His promise, helps us understand, His love controls our future, as He waits for us to be free of suffering and pain… to rejoice in heaven with Him.

Power of Unexpected Change: It is a wonder to me why Americans choose to help other countries, to get relief from pain and suffering, when there is so much need in our own country. I believe it is because " In God We trust," as our motto for this country,. points to love and charity, wherever loom and gloom exists. How we approach suffering, is critical to help others in time of need.

Diverting your problems, to help those in need will bring an uplifting benefit from your actions. However many of us are not capable of doing for others, as we are suffering ourselves. So what do we do? Add others to oiur prayer, is a thought. The question of 'why' we suffer, may go unanswered, as we hope for a quick recovery. Unfortunately, when suffering occurs, we are personally responsible for our own reactions, coping with our circumstances. There is nothing outsiders can do, to control our ability to adjust for change. As we consider toleration on our own terms, we individually fight pros and cons, attempting to find successful balance. When conflict joins our suffering, the reaction is not to dwell on the things we cannot change, but to focus on the positive things we can identify, as a goal to maintain stability and satisfaction. A positive approach to our disability, increases stamina, in hope to capture a better condition. . Physical pain and suffering can be controlled by medications and therapy, but the emotional part of us, will bring stability or misery depending on our response and adjustment to the event. Change happens!. Battling things we have no control over, is useless. Our effort, is to dwell on the remaining portions of what we can do, essential to our ability, then move forward as best we can toward a comfortable outcome. When exposed to a reduction in mental capability, unable to comprehend the battle before us, there is need for accountable caretakers, as advocates, to maintain wellness. Not having the ability to individually fight for compromise or resolution, places us in the dependent care of others, having little choice of personal input. It is wonderful to note, most families are willing to care for their loved ones, often compromising their needs to help. However in some cases, interaction forces separation, due to inadequate means of support, resulting in seeking professional caretakers. The power of unexpected change is evident throughout the world. Many who are consumed by suffering, have no idea of what to do next? Understanding the why and the how of these events, is not as important as finding resolution toward stability and comfort. The point of this discussion is knowing we are on our own. Reacting to pain and suffering, regardless of getting help from others, we must consider our options beyond each changing event.

Stress: Stress can make us question God. If He is love, why do we suffer physical pain or emotional anguish? My faith concludes; God is love, who will test our faith in Him. Anxiety can exhilarate to maximum frustration and if not remedied, and can lead to a helplessness, or a depraved state of mind. Trusting God's will, is a key to finding peace and rest, during difficult times. His choice and power within His will to redeem us, is good enough for me; to believe and follow. A few years ago, facing a situation out of my control, turning to God in prayer, He reminded me to note "thy will be done on earth as it is in Heaven". Because God is in heaven, the assumption of activity on earth, is His doing also. Turning to Prayer, realizing God is ever present, controlling all of creation; giving hope, love and charity, to all who believe. God's will, reduces my anxiety in things we cannot control ourselves. His desire for all of us, is to return to Him forever. Knowing the evilness in this world that can not be corrected by any human being; rests my soul knowing God's Majesty, and His power is above all. God has blessed me, to trust in His will alone, not mine. Presenting burdens, my soul found purpose. Accepting God's will has become a daily process in my faith and communication with Him, as I yield to His presence. God has a purpose for everything and everyone on this planet. Even in pain and suffering. We need to remember, God's will is sufficient in guiding us for His good purpose. The term "let go let God," echoed a new motivation in my future, giving me an opportunity to focus on God's intent for my life, not mine. As a Christian I find tremendous value in "focusing on God." The pleasant times of praying, detours all my anxieties, knowing He loves me and is in charge of my future. Although pain and suffering does drive me to whine and cry out… 'why me'? Then the event settles to a controllable result, and the love God has for me, solidifies my trust in Him.

Help in struggles: In His book, The Bible there are many who have overcome great challenges, inspiring to place their faith in God first. Even when suffering, running toward problems, not away from them, is my motivation. Even though struggles continue, placing my trust in God Will; encourages my actions to move on; with the life He has given me now, and the one to come.. A powerful thing for me, is to divert my negative thoughts, toward positive ones. How do I do that? One of my favorites is to turn to the internet and enjoy the accomplishments of many people who use their talents, in music, or other entertainment, to overcome difficult challenges in their life. Background stories and their talent, is refreshing to my soul. On America's got Talent, the young, the old, the handicapped, the physically fit, and the ones who are recovering from a difficult challenge, or situations provide inspiration for many…a reminder to keep moving forward. As the camera pans the audience, it is easy to see the positive response in these hero's who provide, compassion and value in their accomplishments.

Nursing: Having a career in nursing for decades, both civilian and in the military, I have personally worked in every department of a hospital setting. From Birthing to Geriatrics, Emergency rooms, Intensive care, Cardiac intensive care, Management, Education, Medical and Mental care. During my career, I have seen many dismal situations. The shock threatening life changes, cause negative effects in everyone who is involved. The outcome of any event, critical or not, will test all to consider what happens next. Some dismal outlooks are common. However, those who are trapped in a need for positive change; seek self-evaluation that is extremely important to achieve a successful recovery.

The Grieving Process: Denial, Anger, Bargaining, Depression, Acceptance. Each of these stages need to be resolved to approach successful recovery. The first four parts are identified as a pattern to see if the activity is leading to success or failure. The danger from this process, lies in the inability to complete each category toward recovery, or be trapped in one where there is no breakthrough. Think of this, how many people do you know that are in denial, or angry, or are bargaining, in a difficult situation? How about those who cling to depression? The grieving process is an active part in my existence. It may surprise you to know your decision making can benefit in understanding, using the grieving process format. As a nursing professional, we all agree in wanting the best results for our patients. However, the biggest problem to resolve, is the individual's ability or inability, to overcome their new state of existence.

Capacity for Resolution: When changes affect activity and demeanor, we must find a way to keep going. Depending on the seriousness of the change, it is our responsibility to find stability, leading to satisfactory results. Changing events cannot be accomplished, unless the individual concludes to acceptance. Managing change, emotions may block our capacity to find resolution. Our ability toward sound judgement varies with each individual. Distinguishing the difference between emotion and judgement is the best thought for any change. Our reactions need to overcome, surprise and fear, and summon a resolution with the best possible outcome. Physical changes by accidents or illness create an impact, not only ourselves, but also others around us. Change in our natural abilities, can bring disaster, with no hope, or will guide us to accept any loss, then move forward, under new conditions. There is always a need to compromise, in order to find stability in any situation. Unexpected events can happen at any time, leaving a personal consideration to decide the future. Living after the results of tragic event, is difficult to control, without an effort to establish, a new satisfactory way of living. Depression, substance abuse and possible suicide, may be additional culprits, as we struggle for stability. The most rewarding reaction to change, is when the event is resolved or compromised… to acceptance.

Fighting Change: Proverbs 19:21 NKJ: "Many are the plans in a person's heart, but it is the Lord's purpose that prevails." The God of the Bible is my answer to everything. From creation He has always existed as a loving entity, wanting us to be with Him in His kingdom. As we believe in His word, and accept His Son as our Savior, who paid the debt of our sin, we will find peace and everlasting life. The simple act of believing in God's word, will change your perception about the direction this world is going; gaining much hope in the perfect one to come. Life is not controlled by mankind, but by the power of God and His will. We are helpless to prevent or control our destiny beyond… God's will, wisdom, and power. There are many people living with heavy burdens, distressed by a dismal outlook, having little hope of change. Surprisingly the poor have the ability to endure with what they have, because their life has never been given the opportunity to change for a better future. Why does God allow pain and suffering, as He claims to be a God of love? Think of this… God turned away from His Son for a brief moment, as Jesus consumed the judgement of our sin; enduring with severe brutality, to save our souls. The sacrifice of Jesus, God as the Holy of Holies kept his promise in sending the

Messiah, for the purpose of consuming our sin., as predicted centuries earlier by prophecy!

The Godhead is the Holy of Holies: Jesus, also being God, is the sacrificial lamb, removing the judgement of our sin forever. By believing in His salvation, we are purified in righteousness and able to enter heaven. The Holy Spirit, as the third person in our triune God, gives all believers a connection to God and Jesus, as we respond in our faithfulness, by prayer and service. Jesus kept His promise to send the comforter (also God), the Holy Spirit. Our sin does not stop as long as we live in this flesh. The Holy Spirit is given to us by the grace of our Father, to guide us in following his lead, to understand good from evil, and grow in love for others. Comprehending God's Love: for all of mankind, the simplicity of coming to God in prayer, about any issue, is to claim His superiority and understanding, He knows what you ask, before you ask it. The most wonderful thing about prayer is too commune with God about everything, good or bad, knowing His power is to guide our life for His good purpose. When talking with God, remember all unholy remarks are edited by the Holy Spirit, who knows the content of your intent; and will adjust your conversation by the power of reason of your intension. God wants us to acknowledge Him, to develop a trusting personal relationship with Him, then live in peace and freedom under His precepts grace and guidance, as we are redeemed in our spirit!

The Red Letters: If you read the 'red letters' in the New Testament, they come from Jesus Himself. The true meaning of His purpose is to demonstrate His profound love He has love for us. His word; is essential to complete our everlasting life in Heaven. **Matthew Chapters 5, 6, and 7, contain the beatitudes, spoken by Jesus himself!** Read these spoken words, as God provides intent of our conduct that pleases Him. Jesus died in the innocence of His love, then presented himself in Spirit, to claim the redemption of all believers (His church). Having faith in "God's will" trusting in His love for us, is paramount in the battle for compromise in suffering. The one who is suffering, is the center of God's influence. How we react to the sadness and pain from any event… is in God's hands.

Life Events: Throughout history, many lives have been lost during conflicts of war, or pilfering. Those who are in power; influence oppression by government or threat. Many individuals have little or no freedom to choose a satisfactory response toward a personal comfort zone; attempting to find peace. They are forced to endure their circumstances; unable to retaliate. Few are lucky to live in freedom, while others are oppressed, under all kinds of difficult conditions, doing the best they can to survive.

Influence of World History: Act of God / Spanish Flu:; also known as the 1918 flu pandemic, was an unusually deadly influenza pandemic caused by the HINI influenza.: Lasting from February 1918 to April 1920, it infected 500 million people–about a third of the world's population at the time, in four successive waves. The death toll is typically estimated to have been somewhere between 17 million and 50 million, making it one of the deadliest pandemics in human history.

The first observations of illness and mortality were documented in the United States; along with France, Germany and the United kingdom. To maintain morale, World War I censors minimized these early reports. Newspapers were free to report the epidemic's effects in neutral Spain such as the grave illness of King Alfoso Xlll , and these stories created a false impression as Spain was especially hard hit. This gave rise to the name "Spanish" flu. Historical and epidemiological data are inadequate to identify with certainty the pandemic's geographic origin, with varying views as to its location. Most influenza outbreaks disproportionately kill the very young and the very old, with a higher survival rate for those in between, but the Spanish flu pandemic resulted in a higher than expected mortality rate for young adults. Scientists offer several possible explanations for the high mortality rate of the 1918 influenza pandemic. Some analyses have shown the virus to be particularly deadly because it triggers a cytokine storm, which ravages the stronger immune system of young adults. In contrast, a two thousand and seven analysis of medical journals from the period of the pandemic found that the Viral infection was no more aggressive than previous influenza strains. Instead, malnourishment, overcrowded medical camps; hospitals, and poor hygiene all exacerbated by the recent war, promoted bacterial superinfection. This superinfection killed most of the victims, typically after a somewhat prolonged death bed. The 1918 Spanish flu was the first of two pandemics caused by HINI influenza A virus. (Wikipedia)

Response to Spanish Pandemic Vs. COVID 19 ? How do pandemic's evolve? Did it come out of the sea and change into a virus? Is it a development for Biochemical war fare? Are viruses developing over time to kill mankind? If so, why do some have immunity, and others the ability to recover, while others are consumed by death? The power of this silent killer is obvious, but the reason behind its presence has no infinitive answer. This kind of situation is perplexing, except to those of us who truly believe God has the power to do anything in His Creation. Maybe He is demonstrating His power for unbelievers to think of His existence, and draw near, receiving the love He has for all of mankind? How would you survive in a hostile environment? Have you ever been in a situation thinking there is no way out? What about the children living and dying in poverty all over the world? What is the point of their existence? Why are there things in this world, we cannot control? How did the phenomenal advancements in history find the intelligence to progress into the space age? Why does life and death happen, in just a short period of time? As a person of scientific background, specifically focusing on the 'magnificent structure of humans', it is awesome to consider "all" life around us. Believing how we came to be, is complex, there are many theories and suggestions to this topic. Having a Devine Creator is my choice! The truth of God's existence is written in His Word. How is it that a microscopic virus can, cause world wide death to mankind; while baffling world leaders and the best scientific minds? The path of this destruction, has changed our daily routines and thoughts. Is this conflict an act of God, intended to wake us up, to know we are created by Devine Intervention., and loved beyond measure? We cannot change the will of God, so we acknowledge His presence with a child like trust, and put our faith in Him! So here we are today, facing another silent killer, challenging the finest minds in the world to find a cure. If we consider the historical progress we have accomplished in the past century, our comfort in daily life has improved greatly! Most of the world, can live comfortably, but some are oppressed and committed to poverty. Consider Word conflicts during the past century, also consider any resolution that has brought peace and trust to live with love with understanding? It seems that mankind is constantly battling evil, with little result of overcoming it. Why is it, we cannot live together in peace? Is there a single individual in this world that has the answer? Is there a group of people that can control peace… beyond the United Nations? What can we do in our surroundings to keep good relationships and satisfaction? Why is it so difficult to love one another and help those in need? Why are there few accolades for doing good; and many opinions creating havoc.? Keeping the good and overcoming evil, is a battle mankind cannot win.

Wars and Rumor of wars: It is interesting to compare History since 1620 when the pilgrims landed on our country, and compare it to what is going on today? Ashe Pilgrims Landed: What was the main problem for the Pilgrims when they arrived? Mayflower arrived in Plymouth Harbor on December 16, 1620 and the colonists began building their town. While houses were being built, the group continued to live on the ship. Many of the colonists fell ill. They were probably suffering from scurvy and pneumonia caused by a lack of shelter in the cold, wet weather. The first major conflict to break out between Indians and colonists was the **Pequot War.** Settlers arrived and began clearing huge tracts of land, which was contrary to native traditions of preservation. They brought with them smallpox and other diseases that decimated the native peoples, who had no natural resistance. The decision to help the Pilgrims, whose link had been raiding Native villages and enslaving their people for nearly a century, came after they stole Native food and seed stores and dug up Native graves, pocketing funerary offerings, as described by Pilgrim leader Edward Winslow.

Devout Christians: The Native Americans welcomed the arriving immigrants and helped them survive. Then they celebrated together, even though the Pilgrims considered the Native Americans heathens. The Pilgrims were devout Christians who fled Europe seeking religious freedom. The result was Indians died by the droves from diseases such as smallpox and measles brought by the newcomers-diseases to which the Indians had no immunities. The illnesses so decimated the Indians that in some villages there were not enough of the living, to bury the dead. The Indian Wars began the moment English colonists arrived in Jamestown Virginia, in 1607, when the settlers started an uneasy relationship with the Native Americans (or Indians), who had thrived on the land for thousands of years. At that time, millions of indigenous people had settled across North America in hundreds of different tribes. But between 1622 and the late 19th century, a series of wars and skirmishes known as the Indian Wars took place between American-Indians and European settlers, mainly over land control.

The United States was officially established with the original colonies' fight to win independence from Britain and the gaining of territories from Spain. Ultimately, the U.S. was involved in **five major wars** throughout the 18th and 19th centuries.

World War 1: The assassination of Austrian Archduke Franz Ferdinand (June 28, 1914) was the main catalyst for the start of the Great War (World War I). After the assassination, the following series of events took place: July 28 - Austria declared war on Serbia. The war pitted the Central Powers (mainly Germany, Austria-Hungary, and Turkey) against the Allies(mainly France, Great Britain, Russia, Italy, Japan, **and, from 1917, the United States).**

The Allies won World War I after **four years** of combat and the deaths of some **8.5 million** soldiers as a result of battle wounds or disease.

Food for thought: It is amazing that the early 20th century and the early 21st century are connected too similar to scenario's, of pandemics, inflation or loss because of weak leadership and misguided in favor of the rich, to control the unfortunate.

The Great Depression: 1929; the Stock Market crashes, effecting Bank and the federal reserve systems, the dust bowl farmers could not keep up with there crops, The Smoot-Hawley Tariff kept foreign countries from competing with American industries. In response, foreign countries raised their own tariffs on imports, and soon global trade began to decline, further deepening the state of the Great Depression, In the shadow of the famous First World War, without the knowledge of wars to come. All of this is evident the beginning of our last century,

THE CHALLENGE OF CHANGE

There were 'twenty eight wars' starting from **1899 to 1999,** along with many conflicts to be settled during that time.

The war in Afghanistan began in **2001 - 2014** Lasting thirteen years. The Iraq war lasted from **2003- 2011** about eight years. **Now facing conflicts in our present day:**…with Syria **2011 -**, Libya **-2011,** Yemen **2014 -**,

ISIS 2014 , and most of all, the Russia conflict that may lead to nuclear conflict!

As we face many problems in our own country, seeing the radical change in our history, where are we going to find the leadership to resolve all of these problems? As you think about it, how much change for the good in the world, has been done for world peace? I believe from the beginning of Creation, God has been leading our entire existence , fighting the fallen Angel Satan., in favor of returning us to His resolve through His Son. Jesus sets us free to return to Heaven. It is by our choice to believe and follow, or deny and be in darkness without Hope and peace

Satan: God has removed an eternal member from His household (Satan), to be separated from Him forever, along with his followers. There is a continuing conflict in the realm of heaven we know nothing about. We know there is a galaxy, producing a driving force, that we are trying to figure out. But there are many questions and little answers to the reason why they exist. However, we do know from Gods word, Satan is in the realm of our Galaxy., specifically using our planet for spreading his evil ways; defying God's will to love. There is a celestial war going on that is not over until the last human believing; is taken to heaven. Then according to God's Word, Jesus will come to rule for a thousand years to retrieve new believers who were left behind, but now are committed to believe in Him!

Si Fi Movies It is interesting to know the advancements in the film industry, during the past century, that captivates the possibilities of other beings, coming from somewhere in the universe. I am intrigued by Si-Fi movies trying to capture the 'what if' story! Things beyond this planet, are recorded in what we can see, leaving desire to eventually explore possibilities. Si-Fi movies question the ' what if' imagination of the unknown in the universe. This provides entertainment to explore fantasy, in what might be; but it does not produce value or truth in how and why we are here.

Observing these presentations as entertainment, there are more than a few to disqualify from viewing. It seems, the interest of these movies are surrounded by the possibilities of meeting aliens, who might have similar experiences in their lives as we do. Some recognize their kind is becoming distinct. Many have a leader to balance their concerns, while others are befriended by other species. Then some unite as a common force to defend themselves, or by greed to take the subordinate cultures as slaves or demolish them altogether. Most of these fantasies involve war, presenting spectacular visuals of battles with ugly creatures, creating bloodshed and mayhem. This appears to be entertaining, but in reality, taking closer look of what it means? Using the character of our world conduct, then making it look like something new; my impression to all the wonderment in life, may be considered as SI-Fi, but I truly believe there is a forth dimension to our existence. The Bible explains we are made in Gods image (Spirit). God is Spirit. Being human we cannot see anyones Spirit (forth-dimension); because we live in a three dimension world. Everything we do is connected, to our flesh and bones, coming from God, who also gives us our Spirit to control the flesh. I call this the forth-dimension. The dictionary, presents our spirit: as a noun: The nonphysical part of a person which is the seat of emotions and character; the soul: we seek a harmony between body and spirit. The nonphysical part of a person regarded as their true self and as capable of surviving physical death or separation:… a year after he left, his spirit is still present. My version? There is a triune God, who created us in love, as Spirits. He is the 'Holy of Holies', and cannot be in the presence of sin. Giving us free will, He proclaimed a choice for us to live in His kingdom, by avoiding a single tree, (knowledge, good and evil)… or die! As the story go's, God kept His promise and the sin of disobedience, alienated us from His presence, to die in this world. The Holly of Holies.; has left sin punished to a point of needing reconciliation. Wanting this loss to be corrected; God developed a resolution for us. 'A Savior'… His Son, Jesus Christ. Becoming as both God and a Human human being, without blemish, Jesus consumed the judgement of our sin 'in Human flesh' , giving freedom to 'our spirit', to be without punishment for our sins. If we believe in His life, His Death and Resurrection, the sin in our lives are removed from being judged after death. If we concur to this event and truly believe God exists; we are set free to be with Him forever. Meanwhile God awaits for the final believer to place his trust in Jesus, who will then return again, and claim His kingdom. Although the unknown is fascinating in thought, where do we really find the truth to our existence?

The Risen Christ, Our Hope: 1 Corinthians 15:12-20 NKJ " Now if Christ is preached that He has been raised from the dead, how do some among you say that there is no resurrection of the dead? But if there is no resurrection of the dead, then Christ is not risen. And if Christ is not risen, then our preaching is empty and your faith is also empty. Yes, and we are found false witnesses of God, because we have testified of God that He raised up Christ, whom He did not raise up, if in fact the dead do not rise. For if the dead do not rise, then Christ is not risen. And if Christ is not risen, your faith is futile; you are still in your sins! Then also those who have fallen asleep in Christ have perished. If in this life only we have hope in Christ, we are of all men the most pitiable. But now…Christ is risen from the dead, and has become the first fruits of those who have fallen asleep." Think of this; Two thousand years ago, time was changed, from BC (before Christ) to AD (after his death) and has progressed into two hundred and twenty two years from that point. Has this world dramatically changing during that period of time? If not, what is God's intent? If the world had truly become compliant to God's purpose, in the Creation of life, there would be no need for a Savior or resurrection of Christ! According to the Bible, Jesus is the way, the truth, and with the offering of eternal life as our Savior. Without believing in Him, the world will soon parish, from its fleshly ways, receiving punishment and judgement for sin… and separated away from God for eternity. This simple calling to believe in Jesus, frees us from death, as we pursue the virtue in His loving ways. He gives us the glory of His Word, to be with Him, promising a place in His kingdom forever, and glory in God's presence

SOCIAL HISTORY / SHARING ALONE TIME:

CHAPTER SIX

In todays world, it seems we take little time to reflect on the past.. Using high tech gadgets in our daily routines, detours us from almost everything. The advancement in present day technology is moving to a faster pace of introspective living. We are often influenced by the use of cell phones and computers. Removing them from daily routine, would produce a deep regression in our abilities to thrive. Why is it, when our routines pause for a moment, we begin to find something to fill in the gap? Why is there frustration when I am in a group that is quiet or silent? Why is it, while waiting for long periods of time, I am grateful to have a phone with me, to play with?. Why is it, when we forget our phone, fear overcomes our common since, to panic, in what to do next? As a teenager, in the nineteen fifties, our phone seemed to collect dust. They were seldom used. Big and bulky, they weighed at least five to eight pounds, and remained in one stationary spot, where they were plugged in. The phone company at that time, provided several residences with one cable. If in use, you waited until you hear a buzz tone, or listen to the current conversation in silence, for possible gossip shares, or return later for an open line. Using the phone, everyone on the shared cable, allowed one to silently listen to others resulting in extreme lack of privacy called,… the party line. The telephone system used many central lines connecting to several houses, providing 'operators' on standby to answer questions, or control emergency situations. We did not have 9 1 1, however we were always able to speak to an operator with our concerns (not quite like Siri, but knowledgable and helpful). Also many phone booths were available using coins to pay for a phone call., with a limited length of time.

Today: Phones are becoming the heartbeat of our personal security. They are reminiscent to a loving family. They appear to be the mainstream of our lives; in a somewhat valuable way. I often wonder what would happen if these toys were taken away? Having a laptop computer, a notebook, the newest phone available, plus air pods, and giving thought to getting an 'Apple Watch'… complicates my life, in a good way. Writing a book, is an unbelievable value to a boy like me. Failing most parts of English in High School, the process of writing a book would not be achievable, without these gadgets I use every day. While when working on my masters degree, most of my presentations were 'hand written', without spell check, or proper grammar. I am very grateful to all of my professors, who recognized, content was the most important part, away from questionable format and writing abilities. Today I am grateful for the use of high tech computers, laptops and phones which allows us quick information through research and questions. Recently, I discovered Siri will help me with just about everything, 'including spelling' which gives my wife a rest, away from my nagging process of spelling checks, and editing.

What is it about these non-human objects? Are they taking control in leading our daily lives? Are we removing ourselves from social interaction, as we cherish these gadgets? Can we spend, one week, one day, or even one hour without them? What if you were lost on an island or in a forest, where there is no service. would you self-destruct?

Contemplate suicide? Or would you consider the natural use of your brain, to figure out what to do next? How would we survive without these high tech beloved ones? Do you know how to establish the coordinates of east to west, north to south without a compass? Have you been trained in survival methods? What is the value of your toys, in a situation where there is little or no chance to use them? The average time we spend on our phone, far exceeds the phone time I had during my teen years. The phone at that time, was only available as a source to call friends to meet somewhere, and have a catchup conversation with family, or get help in case of emergency. It was common to get help and information from the operator, or the use of a printed phone book for independent need. Think about this, in the fifties, if you had an accident, away your from your house, your phone was plugged in at home, unavailable to help! However, there were many phone booths scattered around the area, to place a call in the case of an emergency… if only you had coins to pay for the call ? Otherwise running to local houses was another option to get help. The point is, today's life is busy, especially with parents trying to provide social interaction, taking their kids to go… God knows where, and for what reason? Keeping a phone at your side is a constant opportunity for many situations. Along with the constant availability of the phone, our texting fingers develop calluses, as we text just about everything, to everyone. When not texting we play games, or watch videos. In todays world, both parents probably have jobs, so what about their needs? What pleasures are they giving up, for the sake of their children? How do they deal with the lack of appreciation for their efforts? I am not degrading kids as bad news, because I am a kid at heart, but the parents of today have my highest appreciation for their efforts in family cohesiveness. Comments, opinions, and social interaction can produce anxieties out of control, possibly causing separation from friends and family, leaving social interaction to a robot? Texting and receiving messages leads to stress and anxiety, at any inconvenient moment. This kind of stress, can eventually cause a breakdown if not resolved. Say, you were having a pleasant day enjoying life, then someone sent a message that changed your demeanor from happy, to anxiety or anger. What is the effect on your emotion, for the rest of the day? Emotional change may guide us to react immediately, to block our phone, or wait for a time to think about the response. The question is, do we sometimes react to situations without thinking about the end result,? Or do we take time to figure out a good response.? Unfortunately, reaction without thought can be devastating. The need to apologize might be the only resolution. Most of us are quick to respond to unwanted change, sometimes causing emotions to increase out of control. The value in any challenge is, to contemplate how to reach a goal, as best you can, using your best efforts, and also consider compromise, as a part of the solution. This is sometimes difficult for me, because of a history having a quick reaction based on emotion. Although, improved over the years, and sometimes walking away to consider a response, there were times my temper overcame the best of me. Having a flash temper often overcomes my common sense and values. Now older, I can escape this madness, adjusting to strength or weakness. Sometimes the weakness can take your strength away, but if you remain strong, having power to overturn your situation with kindness, follows the intent of Gods love. Weak or strong, self-reflection is essential in overcoming the variety of changes effecting our lives on a daily basis. Sometimes it is good, sometimes it is bad. We seem to do well in things we can accomplish, but what about those times when the remedy is not so easy? Or a change has forced us to regroup into something different from our normal routine ?

During the past; there were times I did not reflect on something that bothered me. Today, we are so bombarded with high tech toys and fast pace living, it is a wonder how we can keep up? Many of us in the older generation, seem to have our eyes wide open, in a frozen look, thinking, what is going on in this age of fast paced living? Relief from this space age, is finding a quiet place, away from the kaos; giving our toys opportunity to reflect on the simple things in life, that do not require answers. Self-evaluation is needed to find adjustment to emotional circumstances, setting time aside for yourself, is refreshing to the soul. Some might say; " how can I set time to relax, when I don't have any time?" Down time is essential in allowing us to ponder the simple things in life. Things that do not require any effort, but only pleasant thoughts. Downtime: Sitting on a beach watching the waves come to shore, considering how the inhabitants in this environment thrive, creates-positive energy form the act of nature. Setting aside time each day, to contemplate life, can bring ideas which may improve our daily routines or allow us rest enough to press on in comfort. So make time in your day, consider your demeanor, and willingness to make a change for the better. Most of all, quiet time can bring a wealth of peace and relaxation. Just by closing your eyes and thinking of pleasant thoughts, your emotions may calm into a restful nap. Being alone, for a comfortable period of time, is beneficial in regrouping your pleasant self. Understanding the value in your life, away from the stress and strain, is essential to your well being. Adjusting to a slower pace, the benefit is to relax and discover that a good time out… is valuable! If not, try to pinpoint why relaxation is not available? Share your concerns with loved ones. There are many scenarios why self evaluation and rest are not beneficial. In some cases, you may need a professional consultant, to give you some happy pills that will safely lift your demeanor. Years ago, my wife, asked my doctor to order Zoloft, an antidepressant, to calm my nerves…and it worked.! I have not cried sense taking that first pill, and did not need a stronger dose, leaving my wife satisfied with the results.

The point is, take some time to establish peace in the hectic live around you. Years ago, intrigued by the concept, to improve social interaction, I found "The Johari Window", which was originally used to improve interpersonal communications and teamwork. This captured my mind, to observe how, or if this works?

The Windows of Known and Unknown:

Psychologists, Joseph Luft and Harrington Ingham, in 1955. Self Evaluation and Strategic insight of…The Johari Window:

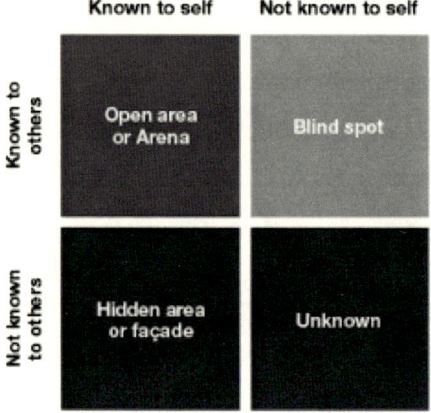

The Johari Window provides an opportunity for self-awareness and trust. Building to be more forthcoming and transparent, as we solicit feedback through a process of self-discovery. Each of the above windows provide interesting information in human interaction.

Four Windows

1. One idea behind the Johari Window is that we all have '**blind spots**', unknown to us, but known to others. If we

want to diminish these blind spots, in order to find more about ourselves, we can only be successful, if we seek truthful feedback from others.

2. We also have information about ourselves that we hold back from others, who are not aware of as, **'hidden from others'**

3. In general society, contact is made in discussing things, '**known to both self and others'.**

4. The last window seems to establish the **'unknown to all'**

Taking time to reflect on self, may or may not help. If we can ignore the consequences of the above blind spot, and trust others with our hidden emotions, it may lead us to knowledge, and the truth of a life. Looking at the 'unknown to all window, we can deduce that three windows are known by self or others. But the last one, is indicating… unknown to all. This is my reason to make the point in having a spiritual being; 'God!' God's presence, is known as my Creator, but not known to all. This reveals there are others who do not know or believe in, an outside source that is maintaining balance in our life, because they do not identify 'God'… as known.'. About the unknown, there is something known to many, as the presence of God. The God who allowed the converted Jewish leader Paul, (among others) to proclaim Him as our Creator, with Dr.Luke, as Doctor and Gentile leader, to record His message found in the book of Acts.

TO THE UNKNOWN GOD:

Addressing the Areopagus: **Acts: 17:22-34 NKJ** "Then Paul stood in the midst of the Areopagus and said, Men of Athens… I perceive that in all things you are very religious; for as I was passing through and considering the objects of your worship, I even found an altar with this inscription: **"TO THE UNKNOWN GOD."**

"Therefore, the One whom you worship without knowing Him, I proclaim to you God, who made the world and everything in it, since He is Lord of heaven and earth, does not dwell in temples made with hands. Nor is He worshiped with men's hands, as though He needed anything, since He gives to all, life, breath, and all things. And He has made from one blood every nation of men to dwell on all the face of the earth, and has determined their pre-appointed times and the boundaries of their dwellings, so that they should seek the Lord, in the hope that they might reach Him and find Him; though He is not far from each one of us; for in Him we live and move and have our being, as also some of your own poets have said, 'For we are also His offspring.' Therefore, since we are the offspring of God, we ought not to think that the Divine Nature is like gold or silver or stone, something shaped by art and man's devising. Truly, these times of ignorance God overlooked, but now commands all men everywhere to repent, because He has appointed a day on which He will judge the world in righteousness by the Man whom He has ordained. He has given assurance of this to all by raising Him from the dead". And when they heard of the resurrection of the dead, some mocked, while others said, "We will hear you again on this matter."… So Paul departed from among them. However, some men joined him and believed, among them Dionysius the Areopagite, a woman named Damaris, and others with them.

What a remarkable change in this Jewish leader Saul, who hunted those who believed in the way of Jesus; soon he would become Paul, dedicating his remaining existence to reveal the power of salvation through belief in Jesus, the Christ. The remarkable Saul, became one of the most powerful leaders, using the influence of the Holy Spirit, with the hand of God guiding his new found life. Now named Paul, His faith changed to the truthfulness in God's written work and his contribution in training others in the way of Jesus. The Devine writings found throughout the New Testament, Pauls contribution rests on proclaiming Jesus, as the Son of God, part of the triune God… Father, Son and Holy Spirit. Paul is not the only one who had an encounter with Jesus, but soon become his servant. There were many saints since the beginning of creation who claimed God as their Spiritual holy Creator. Many stories told in the Bible, proclaim His existence as the one and only God, who has power over all of mankind, giving free will to acknowledge Him and Live forever in His kingdom, never to be separated from His love.

Power:

The world is always yielding to the power of economic pressure, from the wealthy. It seems our democratic values are becoming obsolete as we continue to battle for human rights. The… 'I don't care attitude' of the rich and powerful, want to maintain control of the population, by using any means to get their way, without compassion or resolve. This dictator thinking attitude, is a battle we must face, or be left to compromise our freedom. The power of wealth is still growing, and very difficult to challenge for equality.

Just recently, Canada has claimed this position, along with power of wealth, to control its people, even if innocent of a crime. The power and force of their dictator, has no concern for his people's rights; consuming everything they have, and leave them helpless without retaliation. Also, the Russian Dictator is aggressively attempting to retake Ukraine, by military force, (After removing their ability to fight for their freedom), taking their defense away earlier, makes one realizes how easy it is to re-take this plot of land, ignoring the harm and the deaths of many comrades. In the United States, there have been some in congress who have used their influence to get rich, disregarding their oath of office, many times without sentiment or remorse. They do not consider those who will suffer the consequences. They're barbaric ways. makes me wonder how abstract they get toward human beings… having no value for them, using their control to increase their wealth and status.

God's Reveal: The Spanish flu, and Covid 19, are two reminders of biological items that can cripple the World through the control of the unknown; (I call Him God).

Our triune God created every thing, and controls all that is seen, and unseen.

With this in mind, what do we have to live for? What can we do to stop evil?

United We Stand, seems to be falling to… "do what I say, because I control you"! Think of all the poor nations who thrive with little, to keep alive! Think of the powerless… who will take care of them? In spite of their troubles, look at the world today, and compare it to how it came to be the disaster of loosing our freedom, for greed. What happens when our thoughts turn toward oppression, making us uncomfortable? I am in the group, of more comfortable… but with complete faith in God. Older now, I'm totally ready to meet my Maker, truly believing He is the way the truth and the new life…without all the kaos found in this world. It is interesting to look to the past, and discover the incredible advancement we have made since the beginning years of our World. Wars and rumor of wars were evident from the beginning. However, in the beginning of the industrial revolution, all involved in life at this point, bonded together to concentrate on creating a better to life..

How did people live in the 1880's?

The modern city, as well as the sky-scrapers, (tall buildings), rose to prominence in this decade as well, contributing to the economic prosperity of the time. The 1880s were also part of the Gilded Age, in the United States, which lasted from 1874 to 1907. The United States began as a largely rural nation, with most people living on farms or in small towns and villages. Many of those Americans had settled on the plains in the 1880s. Abundant rainfall in the 1880s and the promise of free land under the Homestead Act, drew easterners to the Plains.

Times Past: Think about this, the phone was invented one hundred and forty-six years ago; around the time of the industrial revolution. Just before that, our country was formed in 1776, marking the existence of our nation only two hundred and forty-six years ago. Then factor forty years of life expectancy at that time. Now our life expectancy is in the upper seventies. .We are more in number by population. and also almost double in life expectancy today. Progress is evident, but what does that mean? According to the Bible, I believe our world is advancing, toward a time when this world will end the agony of war between good and evil. We seem to be waiting for God to receive the last believer into His kingdom, and according to His word, that can happen at any time.

Growth in the Industrial Revolution:

French Panama Canal Failure (1881-1889) Under the charismatic leadership of Ferdinand de Lesseps, the French attempted to construct a sea level canal in Panama. However, after $287 million in expenditures and more than 20,000 deaths, the French attempt failed. The French effort to build the Canal, caused many of them death from malaria and yellow fever. The symptoms of yellow fever were terrifying; fever, headaches, back pain, extreme thirst, and black vomit from internal bleeding. .The disease could progress to kidney failure, seizures, coma, and death. Following the failure of a French construction team in the 1880s, the United States commenced building this canal across a 50-mile stretch of the Panama isthmus in 1904. After being opened in 1914, oversight of the world-famous Panama Canal was transferred from the United States to Panama in 1999.

Panama Canal, 1880-1914 After the United States took over construction in 1904, figures collected on the canal's site show that 5,609 workers died of diseases and accidents. A majority of the men who died under United States management, were natives to the area. Only 350 of the United States deaths were Americans. Why is the above subject important to the challenge of change? When considering the failure of the french, President Roosevelt commissioned an Engineer and a doctor to survey the situation and report if the challenge could be accomplished. This project was important to the economy and defense of the United States. John Findley Wallace (September 10, 1852 – July 3, 1921). Findlay, was an American Engineer and Administrator, best known for serving as the Chief Engineer of the Panama Canal. Findley controlled the project of building better accommodations for the workers and was the major link in the successful completion of the canal. William Crawford Gorgas, (born Oct. 3, 1854, Mobile, Ala., United States(—died July 3, 1920, London, England). As a United States Army sugeon, he contributed greatly to health presentation of workers. The building of the Panama Canal, introducing mosquito control to prevent yellow fever and malaria, and changed other environmental conditions for the safety of all, Findley controlled the project of building better accommodations for the workers, and Gorgas managed patient health and recovery. Considering the challenge in this project, it took compromise and perseverance to be successful. These two characteristics are the foundation in battling unwanted change in our life. Without them we will fail. Physical and emotional circumstances are subject to success or failure. The progress of change can be clearly seen in the advancement of modern-day living. The difference in time, reveals environmental progress, to a faster pace in our existence. The dilemma is how to adapt or keep up on the things that are complex enough to burden us; without resolution?

Flash Forward to Today: What exactly is cyberspace? Cyberspace is a concept describing a widespread, interconnected digital technology. The term cyberspace has become a conventional means to describe anything associated with the Internet and the diverse Internet culture. A gift that keeps on giving… an Android is personal, if we disregard the massive possibilities of having a strangers take control of us. as we innocently use these products that seem to be like something we cannot live without. Even knowing cyber attack crimes, and their possibility of destroying us, we keep on playing with them, because we are addicted to their continual presence. It is incredible, we can do so much with something that is proratable enough to carry in the palm of our hand. However, our dependence may lead to difficult situations out of our control. There are many who have lost identity and the power of privacy, consumed by robocalls calls, or the power of others to track our movements. Many of us know this, yet we take the chance, because of their importance in our life.

Changing Shape:

Modern day smartphones have changed everything that consumers can expect from their phones. The market has transformed the phone into a virtual toolbox with a solution for almost every need. It's not just the technology of the cell phone that has changed over time, the physical design of computers have also gone through a rollercoaster of changes. Original car phones and bag phones were large and heavy.

Modern day computers of today called laptops or note books are light and easy to use.. But as we continue improving these toys, the Phone has become the leader of them all. Some feel cell phones of the future will be adapted to appeal more to our emotional senses. Believing in the future, cell phones will become even more naturally in sync with our biological reflexes and processes such as eye movement, thought processes, kinesthetic, and cultural preferences. It's not just about how we will change cell phones; the question is, how will the cell phone change us?" Just five years after reading this article, look at where we are today? Not only are we getting deeper in the need for these gadgets, we also, may be ignoring the powerful control of cyber companies, who have invaded our privacy, having the additional option of omitting or re-arranging events (able to hide the truth). There are some wonderful opportunities in surfing the web, but I am very concerned about the manipulation of our minds, that steer us in the wrong direction. Are we loosing the chance to hear both sides of media issues being reported in the news? Without reporting Pro's and Con's together, our future is being jeopardized, by lack of truth. Without freedom, we are headed in the direction of oppression, and control, under the sake of power. Without protection in free will, our United States will fall into the hands of evil. It is obvious that the world is influencing change! What would it be like, to be without the benefit of using our futuristic toy's, Or be removed from the freedom to choose our direction in life.?

A Secure way of living:

The design of all living creatures in size, color and purpose, is spellbinding. Some species are related in similar categories by their uniqueness; like dogs and cats; along with other animals we call pets. Most of us would like to have a conversation with our pets on their behavior, but they escape any retribution, by their loving attentive character, beyond the ability to speak. Pets seem to give us a value in simple living, needing to be fed and cared for. In return their unique existence to uplifts our spirit, creating a wonderful bond of love for many. Beyond our ability to have pets, God has established a systematic system to maintain procreation in all living things. The food chain for animals has a long list, as well as insects and vegetation. The purpose for this system is to maintain balance in nature. It is always sad for me to see a predator capture its prey, consuming their lives, in exchange for their own survival. However, without this system, the balance of nature would fail to exist. God created all things! He has designed humans to be the dominant power, controlling our world, then eventually return to Him. However by free choice, to enter His kingdom with everlasting life, many will refuse to know Him.

God petitions us from His Word, to understand His calling of companionship. If we do not acknowledge God through faith, our life is meaningless.

Live through others:
The struggles we face in life are temporary. Recalling heavens time compared to earth time, a life of eighty-two years on this planet is only two hours in Heavens time. Living a very slow pace compared to heaven, our time on earth is very short compared to eternal life. Surround yourself with those in your life, by sharing in events and stories, present to or past, to bring uplifting memories. Conversations, with humor or funny experiences, will definitely lift spirits, away from current troubles; benefiting all, even for a moment. Connect to the world around you, seek a place away from negative thoughts, toward positive opportunities. There are many ways to combat changes, unfortunately a standard plan of care to find comfort in our suffering… does not exist. Each of us, as individuals, must face the situation

independently. There are many who will offer their opinions, like the friends of Job in the Bible; however, the response to our situation, is in our hands to decide the outcome of events in the future. When suffering; a sense there is no escape, is common, and can lead to a despondent outcome. The fight to move on, depends on your condition physically; but also spiritually as well. Having a positive approach in adjusting to your condition, is a key to accepting your transformation as is. For me, God is my answer to everything. From creation until now, He has always existed as a loving entity, wanting us to be in His kingdom. Believing in His word, I cry out with all my trust in Him.… His love is sufficient! However, if physical and emotional discomfort is present, the challenge in remaining faithful, depends on the severity of my pain and suffering, which often tests my commitment to trust God. Praying for endurance, receiving emotional support, or a cure, becomes routine as we turn to God for help. For some of us, our cry seems to go unanswered. Why is that?

Turning to God's Word:

My son David, is pastor of Calvary Chapel Spokane Valley, Washington. We are blessed by his teaching the word of God. Using the Bible, referencing book by book, chapter by chapter, page by page, is encouraging everyone to read and consume God's written intent. All who believe in His Son, will live in His Kingdom forever with prosperity and peace. During my son's twenty five years of tenure, topical sermons are rare. Teaching directly from God's word, is a reliable source to grow our individual faith in God. Using guest speakers, on occasion, is an encouraging way to promote the value in knowing Jesus is everywhere. If a church does not regard Jesus Christ as the Way, he truth, and the Life; that Church is dead!

The Bible follows God's intent to understand there is everlasting life for all who believe in Him. .Each one of us, who fund Jesus, should share or faith with concern for others. Using a gentle spirit to befriend them, with a servants heart, building confidence toward trust in a meaningful relationship, binding us together in Christ. All believers are commissioned to spread the good news from God; as Jesus. welcomes us in His Kingdom through our belief. Sharing may seem difficult, but when the opportunity presents itself, the testimony of the believer, is a great way to begin. One of my favorite things to share is the fact, 'I know Jesus'. Whenever having a brief contact with others or strangers, I try to enlighten them using humor and sincerity, to share how much I need Jesus to guide me away from my stupidity. His graceful power to forgive me, and grow me in His ways, brings much joy by His commitment to love all of mankind, who acknowledges His deity, His sacrifice to save… as God Himself. The fruit of the Spirit is love, joy, peace, long-suffering, kindness, goodness, faithfulness, gentleness, and self control. We can spoil the fruit by our own sin, therefore the need to inform others the value of reconciliation is important. Our fruit might be tainted because of the inevitable sin in our flesh, but the truth is, as we believe in Jesus, reconciling our misdeeds in His presence, we should boldly share the excitement; knowing God's love and forgiveness, is always present. Pastor / Preacher / Teacher:/ Believer: The Pastor is responsible to teach from the Bible, to prepare us to share the love of God with others, using His Word. Our testimony and serving others, is a wonderful way for us to demonstrate God's will to love others, as He loves us, by sharing the truth. The Pastors responsibility is to truthfully present God's Word, and also maintain the elements of need in church activity. His personal involvement, is guiding his flock to understand the power of God's Word. How to spread the good news to others, using God's word as an example, the best way to reveal

Jesus to an unbelievers, is through your testimony. A pastor can be overwhelmed from preaching, and can possibly become exhausted with other events requiring his attention. Most Pastors work more than a 40 hour week. Some spend over 55 hours or more in weekly church projects, and consulting with individuals. Some churches have Associate Pastors, or children Ministry directors, helping to maintain needs of the church, along with volunteers, to help in church activities. However, the burden as a leader, to maintain the integrity of the will of God, is a heavy burden for a committed Pastor commits His life to teach the gospel. Opinions toward church function can overwhelm a leader committed to God's Word, in favor of God's intent, rather than an opinion not established in the Bible.

How long does the average pastor stay in ministry? The average stay at a church for a senior pastor is about four years! Youth pastors last about three! This constant leaving, makes churches doubt active pastors. Small churches feel like they are stepping stones to larger churches". May 28, 2019 Google

There are two common reasons a Pastor would leave the Church. It is obvious, burn-out, can weigh heavily on the mental and physical challenge. Volunteers are helpful and valuable in serving the needs of the church, blessed by their servants hearts; until… they change from serving, too suggesting, or even disagreeing in the direction of the Church, sometimes not according to the Bible. The pastor's responsibility is blessed by God. In the process of preparing the congregation to follow the truth, using the truthful will of God, through His Word, which is ordained by God Himself.! The threat of someone leaving the church 'or else', is difficult… but the burden of blame is always on the pastor, innocent or not. Responsibility for all the Believers is too maintain the flow of what God says in scripture. The responsibility for believers is to share the Heart of God's Word, to everyone who will listen, and be available for their needs to understand the presence of our Loving God.

When there is conflict, with those who have deep opinions on how the church should function, especially away from Biblical truth., need to be corrected. It is important to discuss all issues openly, in agreement, or separate from the church. Threats by individuals, or groups leaving the Church, is an on going process. What we need to do in accomplishing our faith, is having the absolute conviction to Jesus as our Lord and Savior. He leads us to everlasting life. If you read the red letters of the Bible, Jesus (God) is speaking directly to us: as Himself. Matthew chapters 5, 6, and 7, they are the beatitudes spoken by Jesus himself. My repeated encounter with these passages, is God speaking from His written word, imparting us to love and serve, with integrity without conflict or blame. The process of anti-God tactics from the realm of satan, is already defeated by the shed blood of Jesus, who is the authority of all. The responsibility in teaching God's Word is evident throughout the Bible. The Holy Spirit leads many to share the good news , as believers, in the truth in of Jesus. Called by God or not, the value of being a believer or Pastor, is to teach using the Gospel, sharing the Bible with others. Giving the opportunity for others to find salvation in Jesus, the goal is; to avoid a permanent separation in the darkness of Hell.

Pastor David: My son was called at a young age, after escaping from misdirection in his teens. As true believer in the God of the Bible, encouraged by his Sister who reached out to him to read the Bible; His life changed a little before mine, and he headed to Chuck Smith's Calvary Chapel School of Ministry in California. After graduating, he came back to Spokane, teaching as a youth pastor, in North Calvary Chapel, hoping to eventually became a senior pastor of a Church. After serving the Youth for some time, with his wife Colleen at his side, He applied to serve in a small church a few blocks from our Home. The church body was split, by apposing opinions in the congregation. the remaining few, convinced to keep their place of worship, .began the process of finding a new pastor. Eventually David was selected as a senior pastor.Rebuilding a congregation took time, but a few years later, a large group of friends and family, left the church in an unknown dispute. Because of this event, I feared my son would leave because of the situation. But after rest and council, his prayer was answered… to keep on going as is. Twenty five years later, with all the strain and burden from some members in the congregation; rather than leaving the church under duress, my son chose a brief sabbatical to find a solution to the problem of Christian behaviorFrom the beginning until now, he has lead us completely through the entire Bible, three times! As a member in my sons church, he has also encouraged me to see his passion of Biblical Teaching. Preachers and teachers, take charge to share God's love, by helping us understand the reason, why we exist in His Creation. The responsibility to share our faith with others, not by words only, but by using love and kindness, to support to those in need. Our responsibility as believers is to share the good news of Jesus, as a guide for others to consider our value in believing in our Savior. He promises us a perfect life to come, without end, filled with happiness and peace forever; as we believe and share the good news to others.

Gods Plan:

I am overwhelmed how much God directs my path of contentment. His Word, cannot be challenged, because of its absolute truth, coming from prophecy and recorded History, predicting truth of events over time. If the God of the Bible does not exist, there is nothing else known to man, that presents the absolute truth of our existence. Using our faith; Jesus literally came to demonstrate His presence, and offer everlasting love, as we believe in Him. What happens after death is also given by God…identifying us as Spirit. Leaving our flesh behind, returning to paradise forever, as we believe in His existence, and the mystery of life is answered in the validity of God's Word. God's gift of life, is for us to be with Him, living in the power of His love and peace…forever. By world's standards seeking to find articles of proof, in what has evolved over time, has produced many theories that sound like a joke. The theory of the exploding rock (the big bang theory), or some ameba forming arms and legs, then crawling out of the waters and somehow turning into human beings over time, does not explain procreation of all diversified life. The theory of evolving, is a complex feature of life, claimed by theory that our beginning; happened over billions of years… which is questionable in the truth of our existence.

Having a Devine Creator; "God", presented by His word; followed by documents found in history; followed by sending the Messiah, Jesus; as both God and man; building a Christian faith by his actual presence; proving the truth of His deity; to live beyond the flesh in Spirit; then Dying as mankind; He rose again as our Supreme Being and Savior. Proclaiming, man will rise in the same manner, to live again in Spirit. Unknown to many, but known to the ones who seek Him.; we will live by the power of God's Word and His truthful guideline, that makes it very difficult to believe in anything else. Father, Son, and Holy Spirit, is our triune God, who created all things, through His Devine power and presence.

God's intervention, is ignored by most of the world. Many are overwhelmed by the fantasies of mankind; seeking to manipulate circumstances for personal gain. We seem self-inflicted, controlled by force, to adjust to survival of the fittest. But true power of life comes from love and service, with freedom to chose your own path of existence, believing God or not. God Himself, is the power of the universe and beyond. Believing in a Devine Creator, even when overwhelmed by world standards., rests our soul. God's Love is for us, to all who believe and follow.

The Scheme of Satan:

Many of us are guided by selfish intent, seeking no truthful recollection to their evil conduct. Disregarding God Himself; it seems the world is guided by power and oppression toward the weak, without consideration to the dignity as a human being. Boasting in their accomplishments, many are inventing tools to probe space and look for an answer to life. The question is are we searching for something as backup, after we destroy this planet? Or can we ever consider a better life, to find a cure toward world peace, and live in prosperity; for all? I thank God for giving me a brain and a choice, to commit my spirit to Him,… or not. Each day is a new beginning to trust God for His loving kindness. The gift of reconciliation and righteousness comes from His Son; the truth of His Word, and the power of His Holy Spirit, allows me rest in His arms, and be connected to God Himself., to guide us by His will.

Salvation:

When reading about Jesus, becoming both God and man, 'innocent and sinless' the mission of Jesus was to suffer the most brutal physical and emotional sacrifice known to mankind. He, being God, gave his life willingly to gather us into His kingdom forever, as we believe in Him.

The Cross:

Experiencing extreme suffering and pain, Jesus removed the punishment of our sin forever. All animal sacrifices from the past, are no longer needed to maintain favor with God. Today we can do nothing more, than to acknowledge the love of God, delight in the sacrifice of Jesus, then seek His direction and grace, as we pursue life according to His will. Reconciling our misdeeds is the ability to love others. captivated by the words of Jesus, to follow His ways… we receive the Holy Spirit, (Third part of the Triune God), being connected to His presence, having faith that is not consumed by worldly influence (satan), because our flesh. profits nothing!

According to the flesh we will die; but according to the Spirit we will live. The Holy promise from God, is to believe in His Son, then receive His gift of everlasting life, believing in His sacrifice, His love, and new life in paradise, for eternity.

Jesus Predicted:

Seven hundred years, before His first coming, Isaiah wrote about Jesus taking away the punishment of our sin. **Isaiah 53:5 NIV** " But he was pierced for our transgressions, he was crushed for our iniquities; the punishment that brought us peace was on him, and by his wounds we are healed". From the beginning, Jesus knew the result of His sacrifice. Becoming both God/man, He compromised his Devine existence, for the purpose to remove the punishment of our sin forever. How can we get to heaven? As we simply believing in Him, Grace and Mercy is given to us, as we trust in His will to guide our life. By believing, we are given everlasting life, after death of the flesh. Without pain or suffering, we will endure peace that comes from God, preparing a place for us, to live in His Kingdom forever. The Bible is full of stories presenting kaos and destruction, providing outcomes to results of very tragic events. The premise and truth of God's word, is sufficient! Understanding this life is short; then trusting Jesus, we will advance to the next life, having the opportunity to pass through the narrow gate into the realm of; His love; forever.

Free from Indwelling Sin? Why do we need forgiveness?

John 2: 15-17 NKJ " Do not love the world or the things in the world. If anyone loves the world, the love of the Father is not in him. For all that is in the world—the lust of the flesh, the lust of the eyes, and the pride of life—is not of the Father but is of the world. And the world is passing away, and the lust of it; but he who does the will of God, abides forever."

Evidence of Decay: As I grow older, looking into the mirror, I see a wrinkled old man. If I avoid the reflections, the image of my youth is in my mind, providing the best image of my youth… but also gives evidence that there is no going back. Creation is to believe all life on this planet remains balanced. The key in understanding the power of God, doing all of this, is found in the Bible. There are many moments in my daily routines of repenting as I build my relationship with God. This world belongs to satan (for now). Having no participation in the Spiritual realm of Heaven because he has fallen away from God. Using evil power, in attempt to gain superiority, to keep all who love and serve in Christ, confused with his lies. Satan will soon be lead to everlasting darkness, for eternity, because, Jesus has 'won the battle' to save those who believe in Him.

As I think of sin as being a dark area where there is no light. Living in the dark, our thoughts may turn to gloom and doom, with little hope of light. In despair we cry out for help to be free from this nothingness situation. Suddenly there is a light in the distance, small but growing larger, it seems to be headed for us.? Elated and freed from absolute darkness, the speck of light coming from the distance lifts our spirit. It seems to be getting closer and closer, as we focus on everything we see. Soon, it explodes the presence of joy to your soul, as we are removed from the darkness completely, into the light. Being grateful to have the despair of darkness removed, we rejoice in heaven forever, with Jesus as our light!

Ephesians 5:7-10 NKJ "Therefore do not be partakers with them. For you were once darkness, but now you are light in the Lord. Walk as children of light, for the fruit of the Spirit is in all goodness, righteousness, and truth, finding out what is acceptable to the Lord." We no longer have a burden to darkness. Jesus consumed our sin (anything that stands between us and God). There is no judgement for our wrong doings as we believe Jesus; who paid the Price for the judgement of our sin, to set us free. If we follow His ways, knowing He is the only source of light; keeping us from the darkness. His powerful love for us opens the door to the heavenly realm, without evil, allowing us to follow Him forever. Meanwhile as we live in this world, we bounce between good and evil, needing to repent to our Savior, acknowledging the need for His presence and forgiveness.

Romans 8:1-10 NKJ " There is therefore now no condemnation to those who are in Christ Jesus, who do not walk according to the flesh, but according to the Spirit. For the law of the Spirit of life in Christ Jesus has made me free from the law of sin and death. For what the law could not do in that it was weak through the flesh, God did by sending His own Son in the likeness of sinful flesh, on account of sin:! Jesus condemned sin in the flesh, that the righteous requirement of the law might be fulfilled in us, who do not walk according to the flesh, but according to the Spirit. For those who live according to the flesh, set their minds on the things of the flesh, but those who live according to the Spirit, the things of the Spirit. For to be carnally minded is death, but to be spiritually minded is life and peace. Because the carnal mind is enmity against God; for it is not subject to the law of God, nor indeed can be. So then, those who are in the flesh cannot please God. But as believers and children of God, you are not only in the flesh but also in the Spirit, if indeed the Spirit of God dwells in you? Now if anyone does not have the Spirit of Christ, he is not His. And if Christ is in you, the body is dead because of sin, but the Spirit is life because of righteousness. But if the Spirit of Him who raised Jesus from the dead dwells in you, He who raised Christ from the dead will also give life to your mortal bodies through His Spirit that who dwells in you."

Sonship Through the Spirit:

Romans 8:12-17 NKJ " Therefore, brethren, we are debtors—not to the flesh, to live according to the flesh. For if you live according to the flesh you will die; but if by the Spirit you put to death the deeds of the body, you will live. For as many as are led by the Spirit of God, these are sons of God. For you did not receive the spirit of bondage again to fear, but you received the Spirit of adoption by whom we cry out, "Abba, Father." The Spirit Himself bears witness with our spirit that we are children of God, and if children, then heirs— of God and joint heirs with Christ, if indeed we suffer with Him, that we may also be glorified together."

God's Everlasting Love:

Romans 8:31-39 NKJ " What then shall we say to these things? If God is for us, who can be against us? He who did not spare His own Son, but delivered Him up for us all, how shall He not with Him also freely give us all things? Who shall bring a charge against God's elect? It is God who justifies. Who is He who condemns? It is Christ who died, and furthermore is also risen, who is even at the right hand of God, who also makes intercession for us. Who shall separate us from the love of Christ? Shall tribulation, or distress, or persecution, or famine, or nakedness, or peril, or sword? As it is written: For Your sake we are killed all day long; we are accounted as sheep for the slaughter. Yet in all these things we are more than conquerors through Him who loved us. For I am persuaded that neither death nor life, nor angels nor principalities nor powers, nor things present nor things to come, nor height nor depth, nor any other created thing, shall be able to separate us from the love of God which is in Christ Jesus our Lord."

The New Man / Relationship by Grace:

Ephesians 2:1-10 NKJ "And you He made alive, who were dead in trespasses and sins, in which you once walked according to the course of this world, according to the prince of the power of the air, the spirit who now works in the sons of disobedience, among whom also we all once conducted ourselves in the lusts of our flesh, fulfilling the desires of the flesh and of the mind, and were by nature, children of wrath, just as the others. But God, who is rich in mercy, because of His great love with which He loved us, even when we were dead in trespasses, made us alive together with Christ (by grace you have been saved), and raised us up together, and made us sit together in the heavenly places in Christ Jesus, that in the ages to come, He might show the exceeding riches of His grace, His kindness, toward us in Christ Jesus. For by grace you have been saved through faith, and that not of yourselves; it is the gift of God, not of works, lest anyone should boast. For we are His workmanship, created in Christ Jesus for good works, which God prepared beforehand that we should walk in them."

Ephesians 4:17-24 NKJ "This I say, therefore, and testify in the Lord, that you should no longer walk as the rest of the Gentiles walk, in the futility of their mind, having their understanding darkened, being alienated from the life of God, because of the ignorance that is in them, because of the blindness of their heart; who, being past feeling, have given themselves over to lewdness, to work all uncleanness with greediness. But you have not so learned Christ, if indeed you have heard Hm and have been taught by Him, as the truth is in Jesus; that you put off, concerning your former conduct, the old man which grows corrupt according to the deceitful lusts, and be renewed in the spirit of your mind, and that you put on the new man which was created according to God, in true Righteousness and Holiness."

Being Saved:

We are an eternal spirit, living in a human body. The human lifespan is short lived. Assuming, and believing from my soul, God is Who He says He is! The following information is provided toward the possibility of finding peace in your life and your future. The opportunity to make a choice to live in peace forever, is found in the remarkable amount of proof… written in Bible. By adding Written History of the World. to the combination of both, reveals true evidence in Biblical prophecy. Physical and emotional changes often create much anxiety, sometimes to a point of no return. In many situations, my faith in Jesus can falter, creating a downward trend, thinking there is no resolution, no cure, no direction, except through the loving relationship with Jesus, my lord God saved me from all my troubles, thirty years ago, as I melted in His comfortable loving arms,. Receiving a change in my life that encourages love, understanding, peace and perseverance. My faith in our loving Creator, now rests in His existence and will.

Faith / Spirit: We all live in a three demential world knowing only what we see. However, Jesus proclaimed a forth dimension. Luke 11:28 NKJ "More than, blessed are those who hear the word of God and keep it! John 20:29 NKJ "Jesus said to him Thomas, because you have seen Me, you have believed. Blessed are those who have not seen and yet have believed," (Thomas investigated the wounds of Jesus, and believed). The union with God, does not happen by chance. Each one of us has a choice to believe in Him or not. The simplicity of this choice is a commitment to a source of love that brings peace, and understanding to the answer of our existence. The unconditional love from our Creator is forever present. He asks nothing from us but to acknowledge Him and follow His standard of love. He wants us to love others as he loves us. By believing, you begin a fascinating journey of understanding what this life is truly all about… "preparing for the new life to come"! The image of God is not given to us in our flesh. We are spirit and will see the fullness of God when we enter His kingdom. The best way to understand or visualize what the image of God may look like; is to consider His written word, then ponder the beauty and intricacies of His creation.

The Spirit Within: Described by God in His notes, a prophetic writing about 700 years before Jesus came to this planet, brings a powerful prophesy: Isaiah 11:1-5 NKJ "There shall come forth a Rod from the stem of Jesse, And a Branch shall grow out of his roots. The Spirit of the Lord shall rest upon Him, The Spirit of wisdom and understanding, The Spirit of counsel and might, The Spirit of knowledge and of the fear of the Lord. His delight is in the fear of the Lord, And He shall not judge by the sight of His eyes, Nor decide by the hearing of His ears; but with righteousness. He shall judge the poor, and decide with equity for the meek of the earth; He shall strike the earth with the rod of His mouth, and with the breath of His lips He shall slay the wicked. Righteousness shall be the belt of His loins, and faithfulness the belt of His waist". Reviewing this passage, it is remarkable to know that the last book in the bible, also highlights the seven spirits of God., as Jesus sits on His throne, waiting to return to us for the final time.

Note: There Are Seven Spirits: "Spirit of the Lord, Spirit of wisdom, Spirit of understanding, Spirit of counsel, Spirit of might, Spirit of Knowledge, Spirit of comprehension in the fear of the Lord ".

Revelation 4:5 NKJ " And from the throne proceeded lightnings, thunderings, and voices. Seven lamps of fire were burning before the throne, which are the seven Spirits of God".

John 6:63-64 NKJ Jesus said: "It is the Spirit who gives life; the flesh profits nothing." The words that I speak to you are spirit, and they are life ".

From the beginning, God created us in His image; ' Spirit.' In this scripture, Jesus says, "Flesh profits nothing, it is the spirit who gives life". Being spirit, our existence is evident. Our spirit is uniquely placed in the bodies we were given; unique only to us. As we believe; we are able to unite with Jesus, and commune with God in spirit and prayer. Committed to Him, we also receive the power of grace to live in paradise; occupied by the 'spirit within us.' This is what I see as the… 'fourth dimension', "OurSpirit"!

GOD'S LOVE IS DIVINELY PASSIONATE:

CHAPTER SEVEN

The Early Church: There are many accounts of spreading the gospel. In the beginning of the early church, believers were threatened, tortured, and abused with suffering and pain, unless they turned from following… "the Way.'" Through the teachings of Jesus, it is amazing how many believers 'would not turn' from the threat of torture or death, because they believed and followed our Savior, who gave His life for them. This the presence of Jesus in this world, He created; is absolute proof He exists

Today we are not physically threatened as the initial Christians were, but the underlying unbelief in others, is heart breaking and sad. Many Believing Christians have loved ones who do not want to find the tranquility of God's love. They are misguided believing in what they see, disregarding the power of what they don't see in God. As they follow misguided living by world standards, without hope… we pray for their souls, to overcome their darkness, to come into the light of Jesus. I was one of those lost souls, who finally reached out to realize; Christians grow to understand God's intent. Revealing the power of

His is love, through salvation; in Jesus He removes the condemnation of our sin forever, as we truly believe in Him.

As a youngster, I memorized **John 3:16**, as many have done. But now that I am older, and reading a bit farther… there is more to our faith in Jesus, as God continues to explain the reason for His coming. **John 3:1-7 NKJ** There was a man of the Pharisees named Nicodemus, a ruler of the Jews. This man came to Jesus by night and said to Him, "Rabbi, we know that You are a teacher come from God; for no one can do these signs that You do unless God is with him." Jesus answered and said to him, "Most assuredly, I say to you, unless one is born again, he cannot see the kingdom of God." Nicodemus said to Him, "How can a man be born when he is old? Can he enter a second time into his mother's womb and be born?"

Jesus answered, "Most assuredly, I say to you, unless one is born of water and the Spirit, he cannot enter the kingdom of God. That which is born of the flesh is flesh, and that which is born of the Spirit is spirit. Do not marvel that I said to you, 'You must be born again.' **John 3:16-21 NKJ** "For God so loved the world that He gave His only begotten Son, that whoever believes in Him should not perish but have everlasting life. For God did not send His Son into the world to condemn the world, but that the world, through Him, might be saved. He who believes in Him is not condemned; but he who does not believe is condemned already, because he has not believed in the name of the only begotten Son of God. And this is the condemnation, that the light has come into the world, and men loved darkness rather than light, because their deeds were evil. For everyone practicing evil hates the light and does not come to the light, lest his deeds should be exposed. But he who does the truth, comes into the light, that his deeds may be clearly seen, that they have been done in God."

My observation of God: John 3:16-21

1. He gave His only begotten Son.
2. That whoever believes in Him should not perish but have everlasting life.
3. God did not send His Son into the world to condemn the world, but that the world through Him might be saved.
4. He who believes in Him is not condemned.
5. But he who does not believe is condemned already, because he has not believed in the name of the only begotten Son of God.
6. And this is the condemnation, that the light has come into the world, and men loved darkness rather than light, because their deeds were evil. Evil hates the light and does not come into the light,
7. He who does the truth, comes to the light, that his deeds may be clearly seen, that they have been done in God."

It is interesting to number this passage by each presentation; totaling the number seven, that represents "the number of completion in the Bible'.

My Paraphrase:

1. God so loved our world, He gave His only son to redeem his creation.
2. Giving everlasting life to those who believe in Jesus, and follow His Ways.
3. God did not condemn mankind; but came to save us from the Devils death.

4. He who believes is not condemned; if believing form the heart and spirit.

5. He who does not believe is condemned already; by not believing in God.

6. This is life, verses Condemnation; light is God; darkness is the Devil

7. He who walks in the light, is clearly seen that they have love.

Communing with God in Honest intent: Following the will of God, as our Creator, is real! Having more to the Bible than one verse… God's message captures those of us who have journeyed through His Word, Finding answers to why we are here, along with what happens next, after our flesh stops living. I am grateful in knowing there is no other means to our life, but to understand the presence of the unknown God; **who is Known to me.** The One who loves us, as His children providing the means to live forever, as we believe in Jesus!" If you truly believe Jesus came and died for us, offering us the best future life possible, then know all of your sin is taken away, as you believe and follow his lead by Faith… to be in Paradise forever.

Believe It Or Not! God's Book the Bible, is an outreach to all who are weary in the direction this world is going. From the beginning of time, this planet has evolved from a new beginning to what we have today. Each one of us has the opportunity, within our selves, to ponder how it is, we came to be, and where we are going? Our short lives, does not have enough time or talents to find the absolute truth. It is only by written documentation of history and the Bible, we can deduce why we are here. One thing I can be sure of, is the time change in the world from BC and AD. Before Christ and after Christ. Marking three decades in the life of Jesus, an innocent man, who's was brutally treated, to die as a pure man without sin, to overcome our fall from grace. Jesus; removed all of our offenses (sin), as we believe in Him from our heart. He sets us free from the judgement of evil. By believing in him, He purifies us to serve, then opens the gate of heaven for us to enjoy love and peace, forever in His Kingdom

Believing Jesus is God: He was also part of the Creation of this planet, in the form of a triune God… Father, Son and Holy Spirit, claiming Himself as the power behind our life, **'why we are here.'** He revealed there is no other God! No other claim is beyond His power, His grace, His mercy, His truth, His love; for those who believe and follow Him, is to be in His kingdom, with freedom and peace

It is my hope this presentation will encourage the readers to investigate and find, peacefulness, hope, truth, forgiveness, and commitment, in seeking the unknown God of the Bible. Finding the truthful known God of the Bible; His presence, His Word, and His reveal to save all who believe in Him , will gather all His believers, to be in His kingdom forever.

My son pinned a note to me about twenty five years ago; I keep it with things I treasure, in a box on top of my dresser, and read it every time I lift the top. This Biblical calling is a powerful expression in the love of Christ Jesus! Read His plea…

Matthew 11: 28-30 NKJ, "Come to Me, all you who labor and are heavy laden, and I will give you rest. Take My yoke upon you and learn from Me, for I am gentle and lowly in heart, and you will find rest for your souls. For My yoke is easy and My burden is light."